Talks on Talking

（美）Grenville Kleiser \著
史津海 杨柳 \译

● 英汉对照

谈话的艺术

百花文艺出版社
BAIHUA LITERATURE AND ART PUBLISHING HOUSE

图书在版编目（CIP）数据

谈话的艺术/（美）克莱泽（Kleiser,G）著；史津海，杨柳译. 一天津：百花文艺出版社，2009.4（2012.7重印）

ISBN 978-7-5306-5138-4

Ⅰ.谈… Ⅱ.①克…②史…③杨… Ⅲ.语言艺术 Ⅳ.H019

中国版本图书馆CIP数据核字(2009)第036231号

百花文艺出版社出版发行

地址：天津市和平区西康路35号

邮编：300051

e-mail:bhpubl@public.tpt.tj.cn

http://www.bhpubl.com.cn

发行部电话：(022)23332651　邮购部电话：(022)27695043

全国新华书店经销

天津泰宇印务有限公司印刷

*

开本880×1230毫米　1/32　印张8.125　插页2　字数158千字

2009年4月第1版　2012年7月第3次印刷

印数：8001-11000册　定价：18.00元

◉谈话本是平常事

吃饭　穿衣　聊聊天……

◉谈话不是平常事

每一次的谈话都是心与心间

自然　流畅　真诚的交流

目录

前言 …… 002

1.
谈话的艺术 …… 002

2.
形形色色的谈话者 …… 016

3.
谈话者与谈话 …… 028

4.
谈话者的词语运用 …… 038

5.
谈话的语调 …… 054

6.
如何讲故事 …… 070

Contents

Preface …… 003

1.

The Art of Talking …… 003

2.

Types of Talkers …… 017

3.

Talkers and Talking …… 029

4.

Phrases for Talkers …… 039

5.

The Speaking Voice …… 055

6.

How to Tell a Story …… 071

7.

推销中的谈话技巧 …… 088

8.

谈话者及其癖好 …… 098

9.

怎样做好演讲 …… 110

10.

给谈话者的一些实用性建议 …… 132

11.

谈话中的“表演性”因素 …… 138

12.

日常谈话与演讲 …… 148

13.

讲给牧师的话 …… 156

14.

讲话人要保护好自己的嗓子 …… 168

15.

演讲者的禁忌 …… 180

7.
Talking in Salesmanship …… 089

8.
Men and Mannerisms …… 099

9.
How to Speak in Public …… 111

10.
Practical Hints for Speakers …… 133

11.
The Dramatic Element in Speaking …… 139

12.
Conversation and Public Speaking …… 149

13.
A Talk to Preachers …… 157

14.
Care of the Speaker's Throat …… 169

15.
Don'ts for Public Speakers …… 181

16.
演讲者谨记 …… 184

17.
演讲者注意要点 …… 188

18.
《圣经》论演讲 …… 194

19.
关于谈话的深思妙想 …… 196

16.
Do's for Public Speakers …… 185

17.
Points for Speakers …… 189

18.
The Bible on Speech …… 195

19.
Thoughts on Talking …… 197

前言

成功的谈话是一种自然、流畅、真诚的语言交流。因此刻意地用一些规则来控制谈话是不明智的，但我们相信本书中的一些建议还是能够帮助人们在整体上提高日常谈话水平的。

另外，还有许多人不得不参加社交活动、进行商贸谈判、或者必须在公开场合发表演讲，那么我们就应该更加严肃认真地对待“怎样说话”这个问题了。真诚地希望这本小册子能给那些急于提高谈话水平的人以切实的帮助。

衷心地感谢《言谈评论》杂志社的编辑们，感谢他们允许我使用摘自《言谈评论》中的一些选段。

格伦维尔·克莱泽

Preface

Good conversation implies naturalness, spontaneity, and sincerity of utterance. It is not advisable, therefore, to lay down arbitrary rules to govern talking, but it is believed that the suggestions offered here will contribute to the general elevation and improvement of daily speech.

Considering the large number of persons who are obliged to talk in social, business, and public life, the subject of correct speech should receive more serious consideration than is usually given to it. It is earnestly hoped that this volume will be of practical value to those who are desirous of developing and improving their conversational powers.

Appreciative thanks are expressed to the Editors of the *Homiletic Review* for permission to reprint some of the extracts.

Grenville Kleiser

放风筝的孩子可以将纸鸢收回身边，

却无人能收回信口之言。

人皆知“用火须谨慎”是有用的忠告，

而“话语须谨慎”却是更为有用的指教。

没说出的想法有时会湮灭在心头，

可一旦说出口便似覆水难收！

——威尔·卡尔顿

说话是人的重要行为，也是他在世间的第一要务；而谈话则是两人或多人的和谐的语言交流，人们最容易从中获得快乐。谈话是一件无本而万利的事，它帮助人们完善所受的教育，为人们种下友谊的种子，培育出友谊之花。仅仅通过谈话我们就可以了解我们所处的时代和我们自己。

——罗伯特·路易斯·史帝文森

听人夸夸其谈常让我痛苦不堪，

那夸夸其谈的人又总是自以为所说的是至理名言。

我只好绕动着大拇指，仰靠在椅子里，

苦恼地瞅着对面的墙板。

虽然希望他那些谬论早点结束，

嘴上却谨慎地应酬道：“没错——真是高见！”

——阿依

Boys flying kites haul in their white–wing´d birds:

You can´t do that way when you´re flying words.

"Careful with fire," is good advice we know;

"Careful with words," is ten times doubly so.

Thoughts unexpress´d may sometimes fall back dead,

But God Himself can´t kill them once they´re said!

—Will Carleton

The first duty of a man is to speak; that is his chief business in this world; and talk, which is the harmonious speech of two or more, is by far the most accessible of pleasures. It costs nothing; it is all profit; it completes our education; it founds and fosters our friendships; and it is by talk alone that we learn our period and ourselves.

—Robert Louis Stevenson

Vociferated logic kills me quite;
A noisy man is always in the right—
I twirl my thumbs, fall back into my chair,
Fix on the wainscot a distressful stare;
And when I hope his blunders all are out,
Reply discreetly, "To be sure–no doubt!"

—Anon

1.

谈话的艺术

谈话的魅力主要在于谈话者之间的相互理解。温柔体贴地关心别人的感受，感同身受地体察他人的心情，并且欣然地谦让对方，这样才会使谈话顺利地进行。

谈话的心态往往比谈话的内容还重要。我们的人格和魅力比我们说的内容更能影响周围的人，因此在人们聚首谈话的场合，每个人的人格特征都会无形中影响谈话场合的气氛。

应该努力提高个人修养，使自己具有亲和力和同情心，以便在谈话中随时都能表现出这些特点。尽管只有极少数的人具备这样的素质，但这些都是愉快而成功的谈话所必备的条件。

伯克认为礼貌比法律还重要。西德尼·史密斯把礼貌描述成美德的影子。迪安·斯威夫特把礼貌

1.

The Art of Talking

The charm of conversation chiefly depends upon the adaptability of the participants. It is a great accomplishment to be able to enter gently and agreeably into the moods of others, and to give way to them with grace and readiness.

The spirit of conversation is oftentimes more important than the ideas expressed. What we are rather than what we say has the most permanent influence upon those around us. Hence it is that where a group of persons are met together in conversation, it is the inner life of each which silently though none the less surely imparts tone and character to the occasion.

It requires vigorous self-discipline so to cultivate the feelings of kindness and sympathy that they are always in readiness for use. These qualities are essential to agreeable and profitable intercourse, though comparatively few people possess them.

Burke considered manners of more importance than laws. Sidney Smith described manners as the shadows of virtues. Dean Swift defined manners as

定义为让谈话者感到轻松、愉快的艺术。切斯特菲尔德说应该用礼貌来装饰知识，以使其在世界上畅通无阻。埃默森觉得礼貌是由一些细微的牺牲组成的。

我们都已经意识到，令人折服的举止与谈吐是由看似普通的、谦虚有礼的行为和对人体察入微的关爱构成的。一个有魅力的人总是远离怨恨和悲观情绪，而且不爱打听别人的隐私。

人们的个性在妙趣横生的谈话中起重要作用。确切地说，同样的话由两个不同的人说出来会产生完全不同的两种效果，这就是由于这两个人的不同个性导致的。

一个人的日常精神状态会不可避免地在他的脸上留下痕迹，别人则可以从他的脸上准确无误地看出他的心态。一个人的声音、态度和举止会自然地、习惯性地，或者下意识地表现出他到底是个什么样的人，世人最终是会对一个人做出确切的评价的。

聪明的谈话者不会轻易地发表武断的看法，他很少批评别人，而且尽量避免使用结论式的语调和字眼。有人说："在谈话中自己滔滔不绝，不容别人插嘴的人会让大家讨厌；说话者如果不是根据听众的兴趣而是根据自己的喜好选择话题的话，那他真的应该学习一些谈话的基本技巧了。日常谈话就像打网球一样，它需要得到对方愉快的回应，而且回应的力度至少要和发球者的力度差不多。妙言慧语、新奇的词组搭配和精心斟酌的措

the art of putting at ease the people with whom we converse. Chesterfield said manners should adorn knowledge in order to smooth its way through the world. Emerson spoke of manners as composed of petty sacrifices.

We all recognize that a winning manner is made up of seemingly insignificant courtesies, and of constant little attentions. A person of charming manner is usually free from resentments, inquisitiveness, and moods.

Personality plays a large part in interesting conversation. Precisely the same phraseology expressed by two different persons may make two wholly different impressions, and all because of the difference in the personalities of the speakers.

The daily mental life of a man indelibly impresses itself upon his face, where it can be unmistakably read by others. What a person is, innately and habitually, unconsciously discloses itself in voice, manner, and bearing. The world ultimately appraises a man at his true value.

The best type of talker is slow to express positive opinions, is sparing in criticism, and studiously avoids a tone or word of finality. It has been well said that "A talker who monopolizes the conversation is by common consent insufferable, and a man who regulates his choice of topics by reference to what interests not his hearers but himself has yet to learn the alphabet of the art. Conversation is like lawn-tennis, and requires alacrity in return at least as much as vigor in service. A happy phrase, an unexpected collocation

辞都可以使谈话大大增色，但这些在任何时候都不能代替生动有趣的谈话内容，过多地使用这些方法还可能会影响谈话的内容和实质。”这番话可谓金石之言。

比青菲尔德勋爵因为口才出众而赢得了很高的社会名望。有人曾这样评价他：“他说话的方式十分独特，如果想转述他所表达的观念就像试图抓住大海中的泡沫一样徒劳。”他的每句话中至少有5个词的用法令人感到惊讶，可是显然其他的词都难以那么贴切地表明他的观点。他说话的样子就像一匹冲往赛场终点的赛马——每一块肌肉都调动了起来，他每段话都表达得铿锵有力、扣人心扉。

据说马修·阿诺德具备了一个善于谈话者应该具有的所有特征：彬彬有礼、活泼开朗、心地善良 、兴趣广泛、友善亲切、妙语连珠、风趣幽默。曾有人问他最喜欢什么样的话题，他毫不犹豫地回答：“我的谈话对象感兴趣的话题就是我最喜欢的话题。”

应该指出礼貌的言行是成功谈话的基础。如果我们想博得别人的好感，我们就必须自然而然地表现出对他人的体贴和关心。不能以真诚和坦率为借口来原谅自己生硬的态度。就如同我们也

of words, a habitual precision in the choice of terms, are rare and shining ornaments of conversation, but they do not for an instant supply the place of lively and interesting matter, and an excessive care for them is apt to tell unfavorably on the substance of discourse."

When Lord Beaconsfield was talking his way into social fame, someone said of him, "I might as well attempt to gather up the foam of the sea as to convey an idea of the extraordinary language in which he clothed his description. There were at least five words in every sentence that must have been very much astonished at the use they were put to, and yet no others apparently could so well have expressed his idea. He talked like a racehorse approaching the winning-post—every muscle in action, and the utmost energy of expression flung out into every burst."

We are told that Matthew Arnold combined all the characteristics of good conversation — politeness, vivacity, sympathy, interestedness, geniality, a happy choice of words, and a never-failing humor. When he was once asked what was his favorite topic for conversation, he instantly answered, "That in which my companion is most interested."

Courtesy, it will be noted, is the fundamental basis of good conversation. We must show habitual consideration and kindliness towards others if we would attract them to us. Bluntness of manner is no longer excused on the ground that the speaker is sincere and outspoken. We expect and demand

总是希望和要求自己的谈话伙伴能遵守大家公认的谈吐礼貌原则。

曾经有一段时间，不论男女，大家在说话的时候都爱使用讽刺、反语和诡辩术，大家都太过直接地、毫无约束地表达自己的观点，社会对此也熟视无睹。而今天看来，大家说了太多不该说的话。在当今的社会，自我约束力也是成功谈话的重要因素。

现在人们的谈话方式已大为改观。礼貌规范要求我们说话的时候须保持较低的声音，说话前须先思考一下，减少使用不合时宜的典故，在谈话中要避免争吵和刺激别人，不应在谈话中逞强好胜，避免意见冲突，不要伤害别人的感情。

麦考利非常喜欢讲话，但他的问题在于他总是选择自己感兴趣的话题，而且滔滔不绝地讲个不停。与其说他在和别人谈话，不如说他在做演讲。他惊人的记忆力成了他最大的敌人，因为这使他能够罗列大量的事例，别人听他说话时，不是感到钦佩，而是感到无可奈何、不知所措。

卡莱尔能言善辩，但是他却屡屡反对高谈阔论。他经常打破沉寂，告诉世人，高谈阔论会带来什么样的灾难。他说得头头是道，所以让人觉得似乎有些道理。他的态度就像花岗岩那么强硬，因此人们并不怎么喜欢他。他狂热地鼓吹"沉默是金"，虽然他从未身体力行地执行这个准则，但他

that our companion in conversation should observe the recognized courtesies of speech.

There was a time when men and women indulged freely in satire, irony, and repartee. They spoke their thoughts plainly and unequivocally. There were no restraints imposed upon them by society, hence it now appears to us that many things were said which might better have been left unsaid. Self-restraint is nowadays one of the cardinal virtues of good conversation.

The spirit of conversation is greatly changed. We are enjoined to keep the voice low, think before we speak, repress unseasonable allusions, shun whatever may cause a jar or jolt in the minds of others, be seldom prominent in conversation, and avoid all clashing of opinion and collision of feeling.

Macaulay was fond of talking, but made the mistake of always choosing a subject to suit himself and monopolizing the conversation. He lectured rather than talked. His marvelous memory was perhaps his greatest enemy, for though it enabled him to pour forth great masses of facts, people listened to him helplessly rather than admiringly.

Carlyle was a great talker, and talked much in protest of talking. No man broke silence oftener than he to tell the world how great a curse is talking. But he told it eloquently and therein was he justified. There was in him too much vehement sternness, of hard Scotch granite, to make him a pleasant talker in the popular sense. He was the evangelist of golden silence, and though he did not

的才华还是不可否认的。

格拉德斯通是一个不会闲聊的人，他的脑子里总是装满了许多“伟大的话题”，因此，就算只是面对一个人说话，他也像在做大会发言一样严肃。据说，在和维多利亚女王聊天的时候，他也会一成不变地谈一些严肃的话题，当女王试着转换话题时，他会急切地找机会回到原来的主题上，而且还总会提高声音、加快语速，以便让他那个话题持续下去。

莫利勋爵的谈话风格朴实无华，但富有魅力。他从不自以为是，也不强迫别人接受自己的见解。他还很擅长遣词造句。他善谈，但从不滔滔不绝。

有这样一个故事：伦敦的10位社会名流在参加最近的一次宴会时，有人提议他们每人都选择一个人和自己出去远足，并在纸上写下这个人的名字。当10张纸条上的名字被读出来时，结果每张纸条上都写着莫利勋爵的名字。

罗斯伯里勋爵被认为是当代最有口才的人物之一。他不仅态度谦和、举止大方、善解人意，而且观察敏锐，见多识广，所以自然会博得他所到之处的人们的好感。他那悦耳的声音使他的话更容易被人接受，他那纯正的口音使他的话独具魅力。他具备了出色的谈话者应该具备的两个重要条件：

apparently practice it himself, his genius will never diminish.

Gladstone was unable to indulge in small talk. His mind was so constantly occupied with great subjects that he spoke even to one person as if addressing a meeting. It is said that in conversation with Queen Victoria he would invariably choose weighty subjects, and though she tried to make a digression, he would seize the first opportunity to resume his original theme, always reinforced in volume and onrush by the delay.

Lord Morley is attractive though austere in conversation. He never dogmatizes nor obtrudes his own opinions. He is a master of phrase-making. But although he talks well he never talks much.

The story is told that at a recent dinner in London ten leading public men were met together, when one suggested that each gentleman present should write down on paper the name of the man he would specially choose to be his companion on a walking tour. When the ten papers were subsequently read aloud, each bore the name of Lord Morley.

Lord Rosebery is considered one of the most accomplished talkers of the day. Deferential, natural, sympathetic, observant, well-informed, he easily and unconsciously commands the attention of any group of men. His voice is said to recommend what he utters, and a singularly refined accent gives distinction to anything he says. He is a supreme example of two great qualifications for effective talking: having something worth while to say, and

知道说什么，也知道怎么说。

在杰出的加拿大人中，托马斯·怀特爵士是位非常有吸引力的谈话者。他知识面广，博洽多闻，因此他可以轻松地驾驭各种话题：政治、医学、金融、法律、科学、艺术、文学、贸易等等。他对谈话中涉及到的日期、细节、事实、数字和实例都能信手拈来。他的举止自然大方、彬彬有礼、亲切和善，然而在辩论的时候，他会全力以赴、激情满怀，在气势上就让对手难以招架。他讲话时的最大优点是真诚，这使他在同胞中很受欢迎。

约瑟夫·H·乔特阁下肯定会被认为是当代最善于言谈者中的一位。不管在日常谈话中还是在当众讲演时，他都表现得高雅而迷人。他是位无与伦比的讲故事高手。他趣味高雅、有丰富的社会活动阅历，这使他成为了宴会结束时的最佳发言者。

有些名望很高的人士在谈话中竭力谦恭、从不显山露水。他们从不把自己的好恶表现在脸上，也不盛气凌人。还有一些成功人士十分厌恶自我展示。据传闻，已故的亨利·詹姆斯生前非常谦和，一个陌生人就算整整一个晚上和他聊天，也不会知道他的真实身份。

有一则趣闻说的是埃默森和索罗晚上聊天的事。索罗那天回到家后，在日记中写道：“和 R.W.E.聊

knowing how to say it.

Among distinguished Canadians, Sir Thomas White is one of the most interesting speakers. His versatile mind, and broad and varied experience, enable him to converse with almost equal facility upon politics, medicine, finance, law, science, art, literature, or business. Dates, details, facts, figures, and illustrations are at his ready command. His manner is natural, courteous, and genial, but in argumentation the whole man is so thoroughly aroused to earnestness and intensity as almost to overwhelm an opponent. His greatest quality in speaking is his manifest sincerity, and it is this particularly which has ingratiated him in the hearts of his countrymen.

The Honorable Joseph H. Choate must certainly be reckoned among the best conversationalists of our time. His manner, both in conversation and in public speaking, is singularly gracious and winning. He is unsurpassed as a story-teller. His fine taste, combined with long experience as a public man, makes him an ideal after-dinner speaker.

Some eminent men try to mask their greatness when engaged in conversation. They do not wear their feelings nor their greatness on their sleeves. Some have an utter distaste for anything like personal display. It is said of the late Henry James that a stranger might talk to him for an entire evening without discovering his identity.

There is an interesting account of an evening's conversation between Emerson and Thoreau. When Thoreau returned home he wrote in his Journal:

天，或者试图和 R.W.E 聊天，不仅浪费了时间，而且有失身份。他对意见相同的观点也进行驳斥，说的净是废话。” 埃默森对这次谈话的描述则是：“索罗听到某个观点的第一反应就是对它进行驳斥，他这个习惯不仅会妨碍社会交际，而且不利于日常交流。”

日常谈话能为人们提供高级智力训练的机会，就一个人的教养而言，阅读名著是意义重大、不可或缺的部分，而真正的文化则是在谈话中获得的。心灵的交流可以开拓思路，增益智慧。如果没有这种交流，我们的思维也许会处于休眠状态。

谈话的修养不仅是日常与人交往的需要，它还是练习公开演讲的很好的方法，因为如今最好的论坛形式也只不过是谈话的扩大和升级版，所以擅长说话的人一般也擅长演讲。

成功的谈话者还需要具备一些其他的素质：思维敏捷、阐述准确、词汇丰富、表达巧妙、声音悦耳——这些对于成功的演讲者来说也都是必不可少的条件。因此，如果你想在成千上万的听众面前演讲，你就会发现日常谈话将为你提供最好的入门训练的机会。

"Talked, or tried to talk, with R.W.E. Lost my time, nay, almost my identity. He, assuming a false opposition where there was no difference of opinion, talked to the wind." Emerson's version of the conversation was this: "It seemed as if Thoreau's first instinct on hearing a proposition was to controvert it. That habit is chilling to the social affections; it mars conversation."

Conversation offers daily opportunity for intellectual exercise of high order. The reading of great books is desirable and indispensable to education, but real culture comes through the additional training one receives in conversation. The contact of mind with mind tends to stimulate and develop thoughts which otherwise would probably remain dormant.

The culture of conversation is to be recommended not only for its own sake, but also as one of the best means of training in the art of public speaking. Since the best form of platform address today is simply conversation enlarged and elevated, it may almost be assumed that to excel in one is to be proficient in the other.

Good conversation requires, among other things, mental alertness, accuracy of statement, adequate vocabulary, facility of expression, and an agreeable voice, and these qualities are most essential for effective public speaking. Everyone, therefore, who aspires to speaking before an audience of hundreds or thousands, will find his best opportunity for preliminary training in everyday speech.

2.

形形色色的谈话者

在我们的生活中，没有什么比喋喋不休的谈话者更令人讨厌的了。他说起话来总是没完没了。大概他在睡梦中嘴巴也不会闲着。说话是他不变的锻炼方式和消遣。说话使他活得神清气爽，好像他活在世上就是为了说话。如果一天不让他说话，他就会无精打采。他不懈地进行说话练习，这使他能很容易就把普通的谈话者远远地抛在身后。没有什么比长时间的沉默更能使他感到惊恐不安了。他有着最令人难以忍受的喋喋不休的谈话习惯。

肤浅的谈话者也同样不招人喜欢。他说的话很多，但有价值的很少。他的谈话只停留在事情的表面现象上，从不敢涉及深刻的或富含哲理的内容。他总是东拉西扯。他可以谈论天气、服饰、戏剧和体育。他的话没有什么实际意义，因为他的见识本来就很浅薄。他从来不认真地关注任何事情，对他来说没有什么是至关重要的，因为他本来就处于无足轻重的档次。

啰嗦的谈话者说起话来云山雾罩、漫无边际。

2.

Types of Talkers

There is no greater affliction in modern life than the tiresome talker. He talks incessantly. Presumably he talks in his sleep. Talking is his constant exercise and recreation. He thrives on it. He lives for talking's sake. He would languish if he were deprived of it for a single day. His continuous practice in talking enables him easily to outdistance all ordinary competitors. There is nothing which so completely unnerves him as long periods of silence. He has the talking habit in its most virulent form.

The trifling talker is equally objectionable. He talks much, but says little. He skims over the surface of things, and is timid of anything deep or philosophical. He does not tarry at one subject. He talks of the weather, clothes, plays, and sports. He puts little meaning into what he says, because there is little meaning in what he thinks. He cannot look at anything seriously. Nothing is of great significance to him. He is in the class of featherweights.

The tedious talker is one without terminal

他只是一味地唠唠叨叨，没有目的和方向。他站起来要走了，却又不走；他知道他得走了，但还是不走，因为他觉得还有话没说完。你本来已经站起来准备送客了，他却让你站了半个小时。他又絮叨了一会儿。他向你保证说他真的要走了，你客气地告诉他不用着急。他却对你的话信以为真，于是又坐了下来，继续说下去。他又站了起来。直到这时他还是不知道如何打住。他的头脑中缺少谈话的“指南针”。他这个说话者就像一条没有舵的船。

也许最令人厌恶的谈话者就是爱谈论别人隐私的人了。他总爱披露耸人听闻的私人秘密，这些秘密在你听来是绝对不应该随便传播的。他是流言蜚语的批发者。他经常津津有味地谈论最新的风言风语。他是添油加醋的能手，他能巧妙地补全谣言中遗失的细节。他对自己的事毫无兴趣，好像只关心他人的私生活。他无聊透顶，但你又不能得罪他。这种人还十分顽固。

还有一种重复唠叨的谈话者。他反反复复地说一件事唯恐你没有听懂。他非常自我陶醉，他讲同一个故事不是讲两遍而是十几遍，“你以前可能听说过这件事了，”他说，“但这件事太有趣了，实在值得再说一遍。”他试图用华丽的词藻掩饰他的无知。如果他必须重复同样的字眼，他便加重语气，配上有力的手势，或者干脆若无其事地进行重复。

有一种固执的谈话者。即使你已经勉强同意

facilities. He talks right on with no idea of objective or destination. He rises to go, but he does not go. He knows he ought to go, but he simply cannot. He has something more to say. He keeps you standing half an hour. He talks a while longer. He assures you he really must go. You tell him not to hurry. He takes you at your word and sits down again. He talks some more. He rises again. He does not know even now how to conclude. He has no mental compass. He is a rudderless talker.

Probably the most obnoxious type is the tattling talker. He always has something startlingly personal to impart. It is a sacred secret for your ear. He is a wholesale dealer in gossip. He fairly smacks his lips as he relates the latest scandal. He is an expert embellisher. He adroitly supplies missing details. He has nothing of interest in his own life, since he lives wholly in the lives of others. He is a frightful bore, but you cannot offend him. He is adamant.

There is the tautological talker, or the human self-repeater. He goes over the ground again and again lest you have missed something. He is very fond of himself. He tells the same story not twice, but a dozen times. "You may have heard this before," says he, "but it is so good that it will bear repetition." He tries to disguise his poverty of thought in a masquerade of ornate language. If he must repeat his words, he adds a little emphasis, a flourishing gesture, or a spirit of nonchalance.

Again, there is the tenacious talker, who

了他的观点，他还是不放过你。当大家已经缄口放下一个话题的时候，他却热切地又把它拾了起来。他不愿离开那个话题，他固执地要你了解他掌握的情况。你也许能够成功地反驳他，但他坚决固守自己的观点，他坚信自己是正确的。只要你肯听，他还会向你证明他的观点。他对此很有把握，你不可能让他相信他的观点不对，确实不可能。他会把你说得迷迷糊糊，最后根本搞不清楚他的观点到底是什么。

还有一种愚钝的谈话者。有理的事他会说得乱七八糟，没理的事他倒是说得头头是道。他没有心机，而且容易冲动；他经常草率、武断地下结论；他弄不清什么是聪明，什么是愚蠢，他笨拙而粗心。他最大的问题是对别人的权利和感受漠不关心。他从不谨慎，他说话从不经过大脑。他也许会后悔，但从不改正。他经常会被原谅，但从不被尊重。

喜怒无常的谈话者残酷地折磨别人的神经。他做什么都走极端，他情绪化地看待一切事物。他对一些鸡毛蒜皮的小事大发感慨，对朋友总是赞不绝口。他说话时眉飞色舞，奉承他人时若口吐莲花。对他来说什么东西都是“奇妙的”，“惊人的”，“极好的”，“了不起的”，“出色的”，“令人瞠目的”，“难以形容的”，“无与伦比的”。华丽和夸张的词藻充斥着他那毫无新意的议论，他简直是不可救药的热情过剩者。

refuses to release you though you concede his arguments. When all others tacitly drop a subject, he eagerly picks it up. He is reluctant to leave it. He would put you in possession of his special knowledge. You may successfully refute him, but he holds firmly to his own ideas. He is positive he is right. He will prove it, too, if you will only listen. He knows that he knows. You cannot convince him to the contrary, no indeed. He will talk you so blind that at last you are unable to see any viewpoint clearly.

A recognized type is the tactless talker. He says the wrong thing in the right way, and the right thing in the wrong way. He is impulsive and unguarded. He reaches hasty conclusions. He confuses his tactlessness with cleverness. He is awkward and blundering. His indifference to the rights and feelings of others is his greatest enemy. He is a stranger to discretion. He speaks first, and thinks afterwards. He may have regrets, but not resolutions. He is often tolerated, but seldom esteemed.

The temperamental talker is one of the greatest of nerve-destroyers. He deals in superlatives. He views everything emotionally. He talks feelingly of trifles, and ecstatically of friends. He gushes. He flatters. To him everything is "wonderful," "prodigious," "superb," "gorgeous," "heavenly," "amazing," "indescribable," "overwhelming." Extravagance and exaggeration permeate his most commonplace observations. He is an incurable enthusiast.

让你十分恼火的谈话者是那种喜欢抬杠的人，他一边听你说什么，一边在思考怎样反驳你。对于你的最正常的看法他也会加以批驳。他最喜欢说："我不这样认为"，"在这一点上你是错的"，"我有不同的观点"，和"你说的不全面"。你说今天会是个好天气，他就说今天有刮风下雨的兆头。你说今天未必是个晴好的天气，他就会向你保证今天的天气错不了。他对琐碎的小事吹毛求疵。即使没有对手，他也想抬杠。

听拐弯抹角的人说话是对耐心的巨大考验。他在一个话题上慢条斯理地绕来绕去。他仿佛在大道旁的一些小路上穿行着，永不疲倦的眼睛不放过任何东西。他舍近求远，却从不厌倦他那蜿蜒曲折的路程。他缓慢而执著地从这个话题绕到另一个话题。随着话题的不停的转换，他思路的方向也不停地改变。他迂回着、盘旋着、转换着，一点都不觉得厌烦。他最喜欢描述一些细节。他谈话的毛病是东拉西扯，不着边际。

慢条斯理的谈话者从来都是不慌不忙的。他有的是时间。如果你很忙，他可以等。他永远都是那么有节制，那么彬彬有礼。他就像是润滑油、牛奶和玫瑰香水的高级混合物。他说话时力求发好每个音节。他的话有着催眠的效果，可以当催眠曲用。他总是柔声细语、娓娓而谈。他从不说考虑不

The tantalizing talker is one who likes to contradict you. He divides his attention between what you are saying and what he can summon to oppose you. He dissents from your most ordinary observations. His favorite phrases are, "I don't think so," "There is where you are wrong," "I beg to differ," and "Not only that." Tell him it will be a fine day, and he will declare that the signs indicate foul weather. Say that the day is unpromising, and he will assure you it does not look that way to him. He cavils at trifles. He disputes even when there is no antagonist.

To listen to the tortuous talker is a supreme test of patience. He slowly winds his way in and out of a subject. He traverses by-paths, allowing nothing to escape his unwearied eye. He goes a long way about, but never tires of his circuitous journey. Ploddingly and perseveringly he zigzags from one point to another. He alters his course as often as the crooked way of his subject changes. He twists, turns, and diverges without the slightest inconvenience to himself. He likes nothing better than to trace out details. His talking disease is discursiveness.

The tranquil talker never hurries. He has all the time there is. If you are very busy he will wait. He is uniformly moderate and polite. He is a rare combination of oil, milk, and rose-water. He would not harm a syllable of the English language. His talking has a soporific effect. It acts as a lullaby. His speech is low and gentle. He never speaks an ill-considered word. He chooses his

周的话，他非常谨慎地斟酌字眼。这种人被称为细谈慢说的谈话者。

鱼雷炸弹型的谈话者属于说起话来好像炸弹连续爆炸似的类型。他经常会突然插话。他用嘴唇、牙齿、喉咙将声音传向各个方向。他说话就像在打仗，不时发出轰隆声，爆炸声，重击声，咆哮声，碎裂声，撞击声。他使空气中充满了声音的子弹和音节的弹片。他的嗓门像个大喇叭，那声音真是震耳欲聋。他随意向所有的听众开火，仿佛要把天空也撕成碎片。他确实能喊能叫、高声大嗓、劲头十足。他摧毁所有妨碍他的观点，他是语言上的拿破仑。

思维混乱的谈话者什么事情也说不清楚。最动人的故事也会被他讲砸。他总是一张嘴讲话就乱了章法，而且即使你表现出不以为然的神色和态度，他也会继续往下说。他的话总是很不得体，而且越说越混乱。涉及到数字的人和事他总是说错，他记不住人名和地名。他说的话不是不流利而是不准确，他说的话就像一团乱麻。

好大喜功的谈话者总认为自己是谈话的主角儿。他最喜欢的事儿莫过于把自己的观点滴水不漏地讲出来，然后便扬扬得意地举目四顾。他时常喜形于色地说："我早就说过了嘛。"他觉得他是不可能出错的。由于他自己可以随时杜撰事实，所以他似乎知道所有事实的真相。他常常顾盼自雄，因为在他看来，他从未输过一场辩论。他是既胆大又无耻的谈话者。

这些都是我们不应该效仿的谈话。让我们仔

words with measured caution. He is what is known as a smooth talker.

The torpedo talker is of the rapid fire explosive variety. He bursts into a conversation. He scatters labials,dentals, and gutturals in all directions. He is a war−time talker,−boom, burst, bang, roar, crash, thud! He fills the air with vocal bullets and syllabic shrapnel. He is trumpet−tongued, ear−splitting, deafening. He fires promiscuously at all his hearers. He rends the skies asunder. He is nothing if not vociferous, stentorian, lusty. He demolishes every idea in his way. He is a Napoleon of words.

The tangled talker never gets anything quite straight. He inevitably spoils the best story. He always begins at the wrong end. Despite your protests of face and manner he talks on. He talks inopportunely. He be comes inextricably confused. He is weak in statistics. He has no memory for names or places. He lacks not fluency but accuracy. He is a twisted talker.

The triumphant talker lays claim to the star part in any conversation. He likes nothing better than to drive home his point and then look about exultingly. He says gleefully, "I told you so." That he can ever be wrong is inconceivable to him. He knows the facts since he can readily manufacture them himself. He is self−satisfied, for in his own opinion he has never lost an argument. He is a brave and bold talker.

These, then, are some types of talking which we should not emulate. Study the list carefully—

细看看这份名单吧：喋喋不休的，肤浅的，啰嗦的，爱打听别人隐私的，重复唠叨的，固执的，愚钝的，喜怒无常的，爱抬杠的，拐弯抹角的，慢条斯理的，鱼雷炸弹型的，思维混乱的，好大喜功的等等。我们要避免犯和他们一样的错误。谈话应该让双方都感到身心愉悦，而绝不能令人感到厌烦。

the tiresome talker, the trifling talker, the tedious talker, the tattling talker, the tautological talker, the tenacious talker, the tactless talker, the temperamental talker, the tantalizing talker, the tangled talker, the triumphant talker—and guard yourself diligently against the faults which they represent. Talking should always be a pleasure to the speaker and listener, never a bore.

3.

谈话者与谈话

谈话不是言语与嗓音的竞赛，而是心与心的相互接触；不是独白式的自言自语，而是双方受益的观点交流。

在交谈中，有一些基本原则是每个人都应该遵守的，其中最重要的一点就是用礼貌、认真的态度对待别人的观点。培养说话能力的最好办法莫过于首先让自己成为一个饶有兴趣、善解人意的倾听者。

打断别人的话是不礼貌的做法。这种错误虽然常见却应该坚决杜绝。只有专心听别人讲话，你才有理由期望自己讲话时不被打断；同时只需耐心地等待，你自己讲话的机会很快就会到来。

不要让自己在谈话中垄断着话语权，这是一种自私的表现，而很多这样做的人显然并没有意识到这种自私。把故事拉得太长，或者长时间地谈论自己的经历无疑是很不得体的做法。如果不能

3.

Talkers and Talking

Conversation is not a verbal nor vocal contest, but a mutual meeting of minds. It is not a monologue, but a reciprocal exchange of ideas.

There are cardinal rules which everyone should observe in conversation. The first of these is to be prepared always to give courteous and considerate attention to the ideas of others. There is no better way to cultivate your own conversational powers than to train yourself first to be an interesting and sympathetic listener.

It is in bad taste to interrupt a speaker. This is a common fault which should be resolutely guarded against. Moreover, your own opportunity to speak will shortly come if you have patience, when you may reasonably expect to receive the same uninterrupted attention which you have given to others.

Never allow yourself to monopolize a conversation. This is a form of selfishness practiced by many persons apparently unaware of being ill-mannered. It is inexcusably bad taste to tell unduly long stories or lengthy personal experiences. If you

把要讲的故事删节到合适的长度，那就干脆别讲它。喜欢长篇大论的人往往是让人讨厌的谈话者。

尽量避免在谈话时习惯性地拿自己的故事或经历与别人的一比高低。对于一个讲话者来说，最尴尬的事莫过于发现听自己讲话的人迫不及待地要插进一个精彩的故事。千万记住，讲自己的经历时不要刻意盖过别人。比如，如果有人向你讲述他最近去钓鱼时是如何捉到50条鱼的，你不要脱口告诉人家你有一次曾钓到过51条。

不要主动提出意见或建议。有句话说得好：不费力气得到的建议是不值钱的。如果别人确实希望得到你的建议，他们会向你询问的。在这种情况下，他们才更有可能理解你的指教。

不要积极地向别人推荐内科医生、牙医、骨科医生、药物、咖啡替代品、保健食品、疗养场所和包治百病的灵丹妙药等等。如果你确实在这些方面能为他人提供帮助，那就在有人向你求助的时候再告诉他们吧。

在和别人聊天时钻牛角尖是非常不明智的。如果你发现别人不愿意接受你的观点，那你最好换个话题。一定不要把谈话变成争执。

谈话中应该尽量避免东拉西扯、经常离题、断

cannot abridge a story to reasonable dimensions, it would be better to omit it entirely. The habitual long–story teller may easily become a bore.

Avoid the habit of eagerly matching the other person's story or experience with one of your own. There is nothing more disconcerting to a speaker than to observe the listener impatiently waiting to plunge headlong into the conversation with some marvellous tale. Be particularly careful not to outdo another speaker in relating your own experiences. If, for instance, he has just told how he caught fifty fish upon a recent trip, do not succumb to the temptation to tell of the time you caught fifty–one.

Be careful not to give unsolicited advice. It has been well said that advice which costs nothing is worth what it costs. If people desire your counsel they will probably ask for it, in which case they will be more likely to appreciate what you have to tell them.

Do not voluntarily recommend doctors, dentists, osteopaths, pills, coffee substitutes, health foods, health resorts, or panaceas for the ills of mankind. If you can be of service to others in these particular respects, it will be when you are specifically asked for such information.

It is most imprudent to carry an argument to extremes. If you observe an unwillingness in the other person to be convinced by what you say, you had better turn to another subject. Conversation should never resolve itself into controversial debate.

It is well to avoid discursiveness, over–use of

然肯定，要控制住自己，切莫情不自禁地过分强调自己的观点。灵活的态度更容易使对方接受你的思路。

竭力理解对方的观点、体会对方的感受，专心地去领悟他们打算谈论的话题，并真诚地表现出你浓厚的兴趣。在谈话中要使用合适的语气，调整好心态，并适当地保留自己的观点。

你应该习惯于站在别人的角度看问题。这样你会吃惊地发现这个习惯会使你在谈话中开阔视野，并且使你在说话时多了几分宽厚，如果缺少这种习惯，也就不太可能会有这样的宽厚。最好提醒自己，没有哪个人能够完全掌握某个领域的知识。

和谐的谈话要求谈话者有节制、相互适应、语言简洁。各种场合的谈话都存在废话连篇的现象，因此你应该尽量避免犯这个错误，如果没有什么值得说，最好的选择是保持沉默。

要养成在谈话中能够自我约束的习惯。在谈话中一旦意识到自己的问题，就马上纠正过来。例如：如果你意识到自己说话时间太长了，就立刻停下来。如果你发现自己没有专心听说话者说话，就马上停止走神，集中注意力听人家正在讲什么。

不要总是纠正别人的说法，这样做会费力不讨好。他们很可能不需要你的帮助，否则他们会求

parentheses, and positiveness of statement. Keep your desires and feelings from over-coloring your views. A flexible attitude of mind is more likely to win an opponent to your way of thinking.

Take special pains to enter into the minds and feelings of others. Be interested in what they want to talk about. Let your interest be deep and sincere. Adopt the right tone, temper, and reticence in your conversation.

You should accustom yourself to look at things from the other person's standpoint. It is surprising how this habit enlarges the vision and gives a charitableness to speech which might otherwise be absent. It is well to remember that no person can possibly have a monopoly of knowledge upon any subject.

Good conversation demands restraint, adaptability, and reasonable brevity. There is an appalling waste of words on all sides, hence you should constantly guard yourself against this fault. When there is nothing worth-while to say, the best substitute is silence.

Practice self-discipline in talking. Correct any fault in yourself the instant you recognize it. If, for example, you realize that you are talking at too great length, stop it at once. Should you feel that you are not giving interested attention to the speaker, check your mind-wandering immediately and concentrate upon what is being said.

Do not be always setting other people right. This is a thankless as well as useless task. They probably do not want your assistance, or they

助于你的。另外，人们对自己的缺点总是很敏感的，他们更希望你在私底下提供帮助和建议。

没有什么比控制自己的情绪更重要的了。可是情绪常常会失去控制，从而影响判断。你今天的想法和说法也许并非来自成熟的判断而是你目前情绪的产物。要始终让你的判断力居于支配地位。

不要过分强调自己喜欢什么，或不喜欢什么，就像你的情绪一样，这些也需要严加控制。过分强调的意见反而不容易给别人留下深刻的印象。记住你最好的助手是真理，因此在你表达重要观点之前，一定要实事求是地检查你的观点。

要打消想在谈话中不同凡响的愿望，不要总想语惊四座，这一点有时候是挺难做到的，但是却是唯一安全的谈话途径。如果你确实有绝妙的或值得说的话要说，最好自然、谦虚地叙述出来。如果没有合适的时机说，那就把它保留在心中，在那里它会随着时间的推移变得更完善。以自我为中心的言行是文明社会中的大忌。

有失宽厚的刻薄的话是不能脱口而出的，这是一条十分宝贵的建议。但遗憾的是，人们往往急匆匆地发表苛刻的个人意见和批评。必要的保留是维持长久友谊的必要条件。

would ask for it. Besides most people are sensitive about their shortcomings, and prefer to get help and counsel in private.

There is no more important suggestion than to rule your moods. Ofttimes the feelings run away with the judgment. What you think and say today may be due to your present mood, rather than to matured judgment. Let your common sense predominate at all times.

It is not well to give too strong expression to your likes and dislikes. These, like all your feelings, should be governed with a firm hand. Opinions advanced with too much emphasis may easily fail to impress other minds. Remember always that your greatest ally is truth. Therefore frankly and faithfully examine your important opinions before giving them expression.

Resist the desire to be prominent in conversation, or to say clever and surprising things. This is sometimes difficult to do, but it is the only safe course to follow. If you have something brilliant or worth-while to say, it will be best said spontaneously and with due modesty. But if there is no suit able opportunity to say it, put it back in your mind where it may improve with age. Egotism is taboo in polite society.

The suggestion that nothing should be allowed to pass the lips that charity would check is invaluable advice. It is unfortunately all too common to give hasty and harsh expression to personal opinions and criticisms. Reticence is one of the most essential conditions of long friendship.

准确的判断和得体的话语在和谐的谈话中是必不可少的。谈话中不要问很多的问题，即便问问题也只问那些一般性的问题。应该控制住自己的好奇心，因为人们都很反感爱打听别人私事的人。要培养能够合情合理地判断的能力，而达到这一目的的最好的方法就是注意自己的缺点，并且一经发现就及时彻底地改正。

“说话”这个词常常用于贬义，比如：空话、废话、闲话等。但是因为每个人都要说话，我们大家都应该尽量把话说得准确、得体，努力为他人作出表率。

无论如何，说话过少总比说话过多要好些。千万不要为了说话而说话，也不要装腔作势或卖弄学问，更不要有抬杠、固执己见、好为人师、矫揉造作、吹毛求疵的态度。只要用平和的心态谈话——平静地、谨慎地、坦诚地说出自己的观点，你就绝对不会缺少认真的听众了。

Judgment and tact are necessary to good conversation. It is not well to ask many questions, and then only those of a general character. Curiosity should be curbed. Quite properly people resent inquisitiveness. The best way to cultivate the rare grace of judgment is to be mindful of your own faults and to correct them with all speed and thoroughness.

The word "talk" is often used in a derogatory sense, and we hear such expressions as "all talk," "empty talk," and "idle talk." But as everyone talks, we should all do our utmost to set a high example to others of the correct use of speech.

It is always better to talk too little than too much. Never talk for mere talking's sake. Avoid being artificial or pedantic. Don't antagonize, dogmatize, moralize, attitudinize, nor criticise. Talk in poise,—quietly, deliberately, sincerely, and you will never lack an attentive audience.

4.

谈话者的词语运用

据说麦考利绝不允许一个句子未经仔细斟酌就草草成文。他常常写下来之后，再重写，甚至对一个段落或者整个章节进行逻辑上的推敲，来确保更为清楚、满意的句子顺序。他每天都会写下很多，通常有六页纸，之后这些草稿被毫不手软地删改，最后压缩成印刷页两页纸的字数。

英语散文大师都是一些了不起的勤奋的人。史蒂文森以及其他一些大师就曾花很多时间研究词、词组和句子，他们不知疲倦，潜心探索修辞作文的艺术，最终获得了作家的荣誉。

有志于提高说话修养的人，无论他的目的是日常交谈还是公开演讲，最好学习这些伟大作家的榜样。若想大量积累词汇，最好的方法就是在平日阅读时留意有用的、有特色的说法，然后将这些说法摘抄在笔记本上，不时拿出来读一读。此外，

4.

Phrases for Talkers

It is said of Macaulay that he never allowed a sentence to pass muster until it was as good as he could make it. He would write and rewrite, and even construct a paragraph or a whole chapter, in order to secure a more lucid and satisfactory arrangement. He wrote just so much each day, usually an average of six pages, and this manuscript was so erased and corrected that it was finally compressed into two pages of print.

The masters of English prose have been great workers. Stevenson and others like him gave hours and days to the study of words, phrases, and sentences. Through unwearied application to the art of rhetorical composition they ultimately won fame as writers.

The ambitious student of speech culture, whether for use in conversation or in public, will do well to emulate the example of such great writers. One of the best ways to build a large vocabulary is to note useful and striking phrases in one´s general reading. It is advisable to jot down such phrases in a note–book, and to read them

可以把这些词根据它们的用途进行分类，如商务、政治、音乐、教育、文学或戏剧等类别。

不要刻意将这些说法生拉硬拽地用在交谈中，而应该细心观察这些巧妙的词语，注意它们在写作中的用法，以便培养自己对精当词语的鉴赏力以及对其用法的辨别意识，用这种方法掌握的词汇可以很自然地融入我们的表达。

下面列出的一些说法仅供参考。请在朗读的同时，在脑子里反映它们的意思，并用它们造句。仅仅几个星期，这种简单的小练习就可以产生惊人的效果，你的英文将更加熟练与灵活。

我能真切地想象到
一般地说来
一个绝妙的主意
实事求是地说
全凭天赋
你能想象他有多懊悔
我斗胆猜一猜
难以置信
他看起来神秘莫测
足智多谋
我不愿相信
这真的很丢脸
榜样有神奇的效果

aloud from time to time. Such phrases may be classified according to their particular application,—to business, politics, music, education, literature, or the drama.

It is not recommended that such phrases should be consciously dragged into conversation, but the practice of carefully observing felicitous phrases, and of noting them in writing, cultivates the taste for better words and a sense of discrimination in their use. Many phrases noted and studied in this way will unconsciously find their way into one's expression.

The list of phrases which follows is offered as merely suggestive. In reading the phrases aloud it is well to think clearly what each one means, and to fit it into a sentence of one's own making. This simple exercise, practiced for a few weeks, will produce surprising results by way of increased facility and flexibility of English style.

I can well imagine
Broadly speaking
An admirable idea
In a literal sense
By sheer force of genius
You can imagine his chagrin
I hazard a guess
It challenges belief
He has an inscrutable face
Very fertile in resource
I am loath to believe
It is essentially undignified
Example is so contagious

她并不信任我

总的来看

这是对浅薄的谴责

这儿存在误解

我对此非常怀疑

他满脸困惑

批评得对

举个愉快的例子

活得更有尊严

她对音乐马马虎虎

似乎难以置信

超然的理想

使人变得麻木不仁

无可争辩

有理由怀疑

博得广泛的赞誉

他们是人们心中永存的丰碑

非凡的活力与精力

德高望重却不失风趣的人

奇特而有趣的是

给人孤傲的印象

全无冒犯之意

忧心忡忡地打量

运气真好

投机倒把起家的暴发户

他说话很有节制

通达人情世故

缺少亲和力

I am not in her confidence
Taken in the aggregate
It is a reproof to shallowness
There is a misconception here
I strongly suspect it so
He was covered with confusion
It was a just rebuke
A pleasing instance of this
It lends dignity to life
She has a desultory liking for music
It seems incredible
A kind of detached ideal
It blunts the finer sensibilities
Beyond question or cavil
A well–founded suspicion
It has elicited great praise
They are landmarks in memory
Superhuman vigor and activity
A venerable and interesting figure
It is curious and interesting
Gives the impression of aloofness
Perfectly void of offence
Regard with misgiving
A stroke of professional luck
An unscrupulous adventurer
He spoke with extreme reticence
Robust common sense
Deficient in amiability

彻底结束

一腔慈善的热血

明确、实际、可行的

过分激昂的演说

雄心勃勃的人

平添无限趣味

非常适合从事公务性工作

他们满怀敌意

令官方幕后操纵者绝望的事

蛮不讲理的对手

不择手段地争夺权利

被一群赞赏的朋友追捧

以至高无上的口吻

具有词汇丰富、语言活泼的特征

为庄重的尊严所感动

可笑的误解

为人一贯严肃

虚荣奢侈,挥金如土

极其机敏的人

不容偏执

少壮不努力,老大徒伤悲

过分夸张

极尽夸张诽谤之能事

敌视宗教

危机四伏

我冒昧地问一句

脑子不好使了

奇怪的现象

Done with characteristic thoroughness
A vein of philanthropic zeal
Definite, tangible, and practical
Too much effusive declamation
A man of keen ambition
It gives infinite zest
Singular qualifications for public life
They are bitterly hostile
The despair of the official wire–puller
Blind and unreasoning opponent
Ignoble strife for power
Surrounded by a cohort of admiring friends
In an imperative voice
Marked by copiousness and vivacity
Touched with sombre dignity
A ridiculous misconception
Habitual austerity of demeanor
Ostentation and lavish expenditure
A person of exquisite tact
Intolerant of bumptiousness
The obvious danger of dallying
This was grossly overstated
A mass of calumny and exaggeration
Inimical to religion
Fraught with peril
I venture to ask
Attributed to mental decrepitude
A strange phenomena

那不过是一种盲目的信仰

过度兴奋

真相的根源

在可设想的情况下

充满了有感染力的快乐气氛

冷漠的尊严与傲慢的缄默

十足的轻蔑

殷勤待客的艺术

冷酷的哲学观点

几分伤感与嫉妒

源于无知与野蛮

严重的丑闻事件

自我牺牲的光辉事例

在这个例子中得到极好的证明

被正式认可的强有力因素

约束的标志

完全错误的念头

引人注目地接踵而至

我们从惨痛的经历中吸取了教训

脑中浮现想象的画面

惊人的爆发

柔语安慰

大胆的言论

最狂热的支持者

将信将疑

完全胜任这项任务

非凡的魅力

浮夸的话语

It argues a blind faith
Insatiable whirl of excitement
A substratum of truth
Under some conceivable circumstances
Bubbling over with infectious joy
Frigid dignity and arrogant reserve
A profound contempt
The fine art of hospitality
Grim morsels of philosophy
A tinge of sorrowness and jealousy
Due to ignorance and barbarism
Grave and monstrous scandal
A splendid instance of self-devotion
Amusingly exemplified in this case
Recognized and powerful element
A symbol of restraint
An utterly fallacious idea
In rapid and striking succession
We learn from stern experience
Pictures of an inspired imagination
An astonishing outbreak
Soothing words of sympathy
A rather bold assertion
The most enthusiastic adherents
Mere tepid conviction
Eminently qualified for the task
Almost supernatural charm
In glowing and exaggerated phrases

家道小康却朴素

谈论不尽的话题

确凿的严重错误

字斟句酌的语言

乌合之众的全部特征

喜欢夸大其词

特有的讽刺风格

冷峻而尖刻

对卓越对手的慷慨称赞

稳重冷静

狂热的激情

大自然的狂躁

欢快而精彩的表演

少见而出众的组合

出色地扮演了这个角色

慎重的保守主义

肆无忌惮地违背正义

缺乏文采

正如一位伟大的思想家所言

几乎是病态的敏感

谨慎地忍住哈欠

他惊讶得说不出话来

相当熟悉

独特却令人愉快的

深信不疑

表达得天衣无缝

被成功的光芒遮住了视线

我绞尽了脑汁竭力回忆

Somewhat rich and austere
An inexhaustible theme
Grave and undeniable faults
Perfectly chosen language
All the characteristics of a mob
Given to grandiloquent phrase
Peculiar vein of sarcasm
Froze like ice and cut like steel
A generous tribute to an eminent rival
Cold and stately composure
Fiery and passionate enthusiasm
Extraordinary violence of nature
A brilliant and delightful play
Rare and striking combination
Preeminently qualified for the part
Moderate and cautious conservatism
Daring perversions of justice
Devoid of rhetorical device
As a great thinker has observed
Almost morbid sensitiveness
Discreetly stifled yawn
He was dumb with wonder
Scarcely less familiar
Delightfully characteristic
It was a profound conviction
Greatly conceived and expressed
Blinded by its brightness
I have cudgelled my memory

危如累卵

遮掩失礼行为

自然的过渡

成功在望

非常值得称赞的尝试

完全湮没无闻

获得极其辉煌的成功

仿佛进入了无边无际的大海

惟妙惟肖的仿制品

除非我错了

百折不挠

成了责备的字眼

划时代的成就

貌似胡言乱语

得到真挚的同情

最真诚的

流利而兴致勃勃地阐述

亲切的关怀

彬彬有礼

神秘的气氛

激情满怀

极具兴趣地等待

给骗子以当头一棒

这引起了很好的反响

十分恰当的例子

精确完美

广闻多识,无人可比

善于发现不协调之处的敏锐目光

Exposed to imminent peril
Screening a breach of etiquette
By a natural transition
Splendid anticipations of success
A very laudable attempt
Lapsed into complete oblivion
With most distinguished success
Like embarking on a shoreless sea
A really pretty imitation
Unless I greatly err
Undaunted by repeated failure
Became a term of reproach
An epoch–making achievement
In the guise of verbal nonsense
Received with cordial sympathy
With the most obvious sincerity
Held forth with fluency and zest
Gracious solicitude
Punctiliously civil and polite
An air of sphinx–like mystery
Consumed by zeal
Awaited with lively interest
Sledge–hammer blows against humbug
This recalls a happy retort
Preeminently a case in point
Exquisite precision and finish
Incomparably better informed
A keen eye for incongruities

过分客气以至于迁就

最不可能的

极端偏见的人

谦谦君子

说句题外话

了不起的收获

独具魅力的时新式样

一种无意之中的默契

被迫切地需求

Polite to the point of deference
To the last degree improbable
People with rampant prejudices
A model of chivalrous propriety
By way of digression
A splendid acquisition
Singularly attractive fashion
A kind of unconscious conspiracy
Amid engrossing demands

5.

谈话的语调

谈话需要讲究语调，当今社会普遍需要人们大力提高这方面的修养，但是，具体关注这个重要问题的人却出乎意料的少。无论在哪儿我们都遭受着那些刺耳、难听的声音的折磨，只有偶尔才能享受到悦耳柔和的声音。

大多数人说话时太过用力，他们绷紧嗓子和嘴巴的肌肉，却不是放松它们，让声音自然和谐地发出。解决这种常见口腔紧张的方法就是放松所有说话时用到的肌肉。只需每天做些小练习就能见效。

首先要记住的是我们应该用嗓子说话而不是用嗓子发音。悦耳的声音主要是由舌头送向硬腭或者上牙弓而发出的，因为嘴的这个部位可以使声音产生回响。

5.

The Speaking Voice

There is a widespread need for a more thorough cultivation of the speaking voice. It is astonishing how few persons give specific attention to this important subject. On all sides we are subjected to voices that are disagreeable and strident. It is the exception to hear a voice that is musical and well–modulated.

Most people make too much physical effort in speaking. They tighten the muscles of the throat and mouth, instead of liberating these muscles and allowing the voice to flow naturally and harmoniously. The remedy for this common fault of vocal tension is to relax all the muscles used in speech. This is easily accomplished by means of a little daily practice.

The first thing to keep in mind is that we should speak through the throat and not from it. A musical quality of voice depends chiefly upon directing the tone towards the hard palate, or the bony arch above the upper teeth. From this part of the mouth the voice acquires much of its resonance.

放松嗓子的一个好方法就是打哈欠。当然，不用等到真的想打哈欠的时候，只需要模仿一下打哈欠的动作就可以达到理想的效果。在这里建议大家哈欠练习过后，可以马上读或说上一段，试试嗓音，看看声调自如程度改善的情况。

在喧嚷嘈杂的环境里，最好不要勉强用嗓子，很多好嗓音都毁于习惯在大街上或其他喧闹的地方不停地说话。在那种环境里，最好休息嗓子别说话，因为你的声音一定竞争不过那样的喧阗。

我们在日常交谈中应尽量使声音平和，不要突然提高声调，不要在嗓门上争高下；我们的语言应更加活泼多样，而非声嘶力竭；我们需要冷静而不失朝气的头脑，它能让我们远离生活中的琐碎烦恼。总之，我们说话时需要多一些泰然自若和自我控制。

我们应当牢记我们所说的事情中很少有特别重要以至于非得强调的，所说的事重不重要自有其思想内涵来表达。若是非强调不可，那么请用一些明智的方法，比如停顿或变换语调，可别耸肩握拳。

使用鼻音或“用鼻子说话”是常见的错误，那会令人很不舒服。许多人有这个毛病，却很少被察觉。这种习惯常常在不知不觉间形成。同样令人感

An excellent exercise for throat relaxation is yawning. It is not necessary to wait until a real yawn presents itself, but frequent practice in imitating a yawn may be indulged in with good results. Immediately after practicing the yawn, it is advisable to test the voice, either in speaking or in reading, to observe improvement in freedom of tone.

It is not desirable to use the voice where there is loud noise by way of opposition. Many a good voice has been ruined due to the habit of continuous talking on the street or elsewhere amid clatter and hubbub. Under such circumstances it is better to rest the voice, since in any contest of the kind the voice will almost surely be vanquished.

What we need in our daily conversation is less emphasis, and more quietness and non–resistance. We need less eagerness and more vivacity and variety. We need a settled equanimity of mind that does not deprive us of our animation, but saves us from the petty irritations of everyday life. We need, in short, more poise and self–control in our way of speaking.

It is well to remember that few things we say are of such importance as to require emphasis. The thought should be its own recommendation. But if emphasis be necessary, let it be by the intellectual means of pausing or inflection, rather than with the shoulders or the clenched fist.

A very disagreeable and common fault is nasality, or "talking through the nose." Many persons are guilty of this who least suspect it. This

到别扭的是用喉音说话的毛病，其根源在于没放松而是紧绷了喉咙的肌肉，因此每个人都应该尽量防止这种习惯的形成。

最好的说话语调是中低调，它十分适合日常交谈。高声调说话是缘于个人的习惯或脾气，但也可通过一些适当的练习来克服。高声调的缺点是它不仅令听者不舒服，而且让说话人跟听者“不融洽”。

好的语调应该具备的优点是纯正、洪亮、柔和、圆润、清晰，并且张弛有度。拥有这些优点并不难，只需每天朗读十分钟，每次都关注一种优点。几周后，你辛苦的练习就可以收到满意的成效。声音可以通过使用得到改善，而且要通过使用让好的声音成为习惯。

清晰准确的发音是文雅言谈的表现。卖弄学问不可取，但是想要学好说话，勤查字典是必不可少的。一位作家提出了很好的忠告：

“你应当下定决心无论在任何场合都杜绝不正确的、不高雅的或者粗俗的词句。如果你天资聪慧，你很快就会发现用纯正的英语说出的话比任

habit is so easily and unconsciously acquired that everyone should be on strict guard against it. Almost equally disagreeable is the fault of throatiness, caused by holding the muscles of the throat instead of relaxing them.

The best tones of the speaking voice are the middle and low keys. These should be used exclusively in daily conversation. The use of high pitch is due to habit or temperament, but may be overcome through judicious practice. The objection to a high-keyed voice is not only that it is disagreeable to the listener, but puts the speaker "out of tune" with his audience.

A good speaking voice should possess the qualities of purity, resonance, flexibility, roundness, brilliancy, and adequate power. These qualities can be rapidly developed by daily reading aloud for ten minutes, giving special attention to one quality at a time. A few weeks, assiduous practice will produce most gratifying results. The voice grows through use, and it grows precisely in the way it is habitually used.

Distinct articulation and correct pronunciation are indications of cultivated speech. Pedantry should be avoided, but every aspirant to correct speech should be a student of the dictionary. A writer has given this good counsel:

"Resolve that you will never use an incorrect, an inelegant, or a vulgar phrase or word, in any society whatever. If you are gifted with wit, you will soon find that it is easy to give it far better point and force in pure English than through any

何其他不地道的说法都更有说服力，此外好的词句可以让你的卓见给别人留下最深刻的印象。无论你付出了多大努力，那努力是不会白费的，因为它会为你赢得谈吐文雅的好名声。那些很少有机会同受过良好教育的人交流的人难免会使用一些当今社会不再流行却经常出现在书中的词语。由于这些表达经常出现在小说中，读者应当谨记即使是最经典的小说，里面的话语在我们的日常生活中也常常会显得不自然。交谈中的这个毛病是最难改正的，而且不幸的是，正是那些竭力想把话说正确的人最容易犯这个毛病。这个习惯很糟糕，因为虽然那些词语不像俚语那样本身粗俗，却会让人们觉得你在竭力掩饰粗俗。一般说来解决的办法是当你觉得一些词句的使用只是为起装饰作用时就不要使用，当你感到一些词句的使用只是让别人觉得你见多识广时，就该换些朴实的说法。而当你对一个词的发音没把握时，千万别冒险，即使诱惑力很大也要抗拒。因为，假若你对那发音有一丁点儿的迟疑却又听任了诱惑，你肯定会出错。可以用英语词表达的意思就不要使用外语词表

other medium, and that brilliant thoughts make the deepest impressions when well worded. However great it may be, the labor is never lost which earns for you the reputation of one who habitually uses the language of a gentleman, or of a lady. It is difficult for those who have not frequent opportunities for conversation with well-educated people, to avoid using expressions which are not current in society, although they may be of common occurrence in books. As they are often learned from novels, it will be well for the reader to remember that even in the best of such works dialogues are seldom sustained in a tone which would not appear affected in ordinary life. This fault in conversation is the most difficult of all to amend, and it is unfortunately the one to which those who strive to express themselves correctly are peculiarly liable. Its effect is bad, for though it is not like slang, vulgar in itself, it betrays an effort to conceal vulgarity. It may generally be remedied by avoiding any word or phrase which you may suspect yourself of using for the purpose of creating an effect. Whenever you imagine that the employment of any mere word or sentence will convey the impression that you are well informed, substitute for it some simple expression. If you are not positively certain as to the pronunciation of a word, never use it. If the temptation be great, resist it; for, rely upon it, if there be in your mind the slightest doubt on the subject, you will certainly make a mistake. Never use a foreign word when its meaning can be given in English,

达，因为说对方可能听不懂的词既不礼貌又很愚蠢。任何情况下都别试图搀杂点外语词，除非你能很地道地说那门外语。”

说话时应注意嘴张得要恰到好处。很多人嘴张得不够，有点像咬着牙说话，结果导致声音的质量和发音的正确性都打了折扣。辅音和元音都十分重要，含糊不清的话音几乎跟结巴一样令人听起来不舒服。

从容不迫地说话可以令交谈更愉快、更有效。语速太快会使说话人吐字不清、语调单调和呼吸不均。而从容不迫地说话却有很多好处，至少令听者十分舒服。

许多人的嗓音太细弱，即使他们的思想异常出众，表达出来却没有说服力。解决的方法是平时注意多发深沉宽厚的音。最好的练习就是每天用几分钟练习发元音“O”（噢），尽量将其发得饱满、深沉、悦耳。更加全面的嗓音练习就是用不同的力度和音调分别发这个音的高声调和低声调。

一些人的声音太轻、传不远，解决的办法是每

and remember that it is both rude and silly to say anything to any person who possibly may not understand it. But never attempt, under any circumstances whatever, to utter a foreign word, unless you have learned to pronounce correctly the language to which it belongs."

There is need for the admonition to open the mouth well. Many people speak with half-closed teeth, the result being that the quality of voice and correctness of pronunciation are greatly impaired. Consonants and vowels should be given proper significance. Muffled speech is almost as objectionable as stammering.

It enhances the pleasure and quality of conversation to speak in deliberate style. Rapidity of utterance often leads a speaker into such faults as indistinctness, monotony, and incorrect breathing. Deliberate speaking confers many advantages, not the least of which is increased pleasure to the listener.

Many voices are too thin in quality. They fail to carry conviction even when the thought is of superior character. The remedy here is to give special attention to the development of deep tones. One of the best exercises for this purpose is to practice for a few minutes daily upon the vowel sound "O," endeavoring to make it full, deep, and melodious. For all-round vocal development this practice should be done with varied force and inflection, and on high as well as low keys of the voice.

The best remedy for a weak voice is to

天练习爆破音，同时用不同音调发主元音，并且发音时配合使用腹部肌肉。另一个好办法就是在上楼梯或走上坡路时大声朗读，由于这些练习方法有些极端，学生使用时应小心谨慎。

正确的呼吸方式有助于把话讲得准确、悦耳。应该每天练习对呼吸器官的控制，练习的内容和方法可参见有关演说技巧的权威书籍中的介绍。纯正声调的产生有赖于将所有气息都转化为声调的能力，不当的送气发音会使一些气息流失没起到发音的作用，同时会伤害喉咙，也会使听者感到不舒服。

无论是日常交谈还是当众演讲，讲话者说话时都应有足够的喘息间歇。从容不迫地讲话可以使肺有机会重新充满氧气，而讲话者也不至于很快疲劳。当然，应当养成间歇时用鼻子呼吸的习惯。

有一种嗓音特别圆润饱满，被称为亮堂的嗓音，这是演说家必不可少的嗓音。其音质朴实、纯正，因此声音就显得更为圆润饱满。这主要利用了胸腔和口腔越来越强的共鸣以及腹部肌肉更有力的收放配合。它的特点是饱满，但不一定是很大的声音。它绝非做作之音，仅仅是比日常谈话的声音

practice daily upon explosives, expelling the principal vowel sounds, on various keys, using the abdominal muscles throughout. Another good exercise is to read aloud while walking upstairs or uphill. As these exercises are somewhat extreme, the student is recommended to practice them prudently.

Correct breathing is fundamental to correct and agreeable speaking. The breathing apparatus should be brought under control by daily practice upon exercises prescribed in any standard book on elocution. Pure tone of voice depends upon the ability to convert into tone every particle of breath used. Aspirated voice, in which some of the breath is allowed to escape unvocalized, is injurious to the throat, and unpleasant to the listening ear.

The speaker, whether in conversation or in public, should try always to speak with an adequate supply of breath. Deliberate utterance will give the necessary opportunity to replenish the lungs, so that the speaker will not suffer from unnecessary fatigue. Needless to say, the habit should be formed of breathing through the nose when in repose.

There is a voice of unusual roundness and fulness known as the orotund, which is indispensable to the public speaker. It is simple, pure tone, rounded out into greater fulness. It is produced mainly by an increased resonance of the chest and mouth cavities, and a more vigorous action of the abdominal muscles. It has the character of fulness, but it is not necessarily a loud tone. It is in no sense artificial, but simply an

稍大一些。

亮堂声音的使用需根据要表达的思想和感情的强烈程度而适当调整。当我们需要把话说得很有尊严、很有力量、很崇高、很庄重时可以使用亮堂的声音。当我们在公共场合祈祷和读《圣经》时也可以使用，这样演讲者就可以使公共场合的讲话与日常交谈的风格有所区别。它可使说话人充分发挥声音的力度和强度，从而让声音传得更远、更有力量。

如果声音缺少共鸣，可以闭着嘴发“m”音，同时配合脸部震动来练习，这样会很快收到良好的效果。在整个练习过程中，声音应保持靠前，紧贴嘴唇和硬腭。之后的练习从“m”音开始，再渐渐将嘴唇张开，变为发“ah”音，同时仍然保持最初的共鸣。

说话的声音可以变得很动听。每个人都有责任挖掘自己声音中的美。日常生活中出现明显难听的说话声音主要原因是人们的粗心和忽视。然而，令人欣喜的是，人们比以往更加关注这个重要问题了。当然，说话的声音是人们交流思想的主要工具，对它的完善无疑是至关紧要的。就像斯托里所说的：

“哦，我们的嗓子和乐器多么神奇，发出多样的声音美妙动听！

enlargement of the natural conversational voice.

The use of the orotund voice varies according to the intensity of the thought and feeling being expressed. It is used in language of great dignity, power, grandeur, and sublimity. It is appropriate in certain forms of public prayer and Bible reading. It enables the public speaker to vary from his conversational style. It gives vastly increased scope and power, by enabling the speaker to bring into play all the resources of vocal force and intensity.

Where resonance of voice is lacking, it can be rapidly developed by means of humming the letter "m", with lips closed, and endeavoring to make the face vibrate. The tone should be kept well forward throughout the exercise, pressing firmly against the lips and hard palate. Later the exercise may begin with the humming "m", and be developed, while the lips are opened gradually, into the tone of "ah", still aiming to maintain the original resonance.

The speaking voice is capable of most wonderful development. There is a duty devolving upon everyone to cultivate beauty of vocal utterance and diction. Crudities of speech so commonly in evidence are mainly due to carelessness and neglect. It is a hopeful sign, however, that greater attention is now being given to this important subject than heretofore. Surely there is nothing more important than the development of the principal instrument by which men communicate with one another. As Story says:

"O, how our organ can speak with its many and wonderful voices!—

诗琴曼奏歌颂爱情，号角猛吹催促出征，

高高的音调，唱出饱满的和音。

风琴脚键盘踩踩停停，空气也随之颤动。”

Play on the soft lute of love, blow the loud trumpet of war,

Sing with the high sesquialter, or, drawing its full diapason,

Shake all the air with the grand storm of its pedals and stops."

6.

如何讲故事

有人曾诙谐地说只有那些步入老年、好谈往事的人才应该讲故事，德昆西则希望把所有爱讲故事的人都泡在洗马池中，或者把他们都当作疯狗。然而讲故事有其合情合理的作用，如果遵循一定的规则去讲故事，则会为日常交谈或公开演讲增色不少。

我们要善于把握讲故事的时机，如果时机不对，即使你的故事就在嘴边也不要去冒险。很少有人把握得好什么场合该讲什么故事。很多人爱讲故事，但那些故事却冗长、平淡、无趣，让人难以忍受。

我们大概都见识过那种演讲者，其开场白是："我并不想讲烦人的长故事，但是这个故事的确很棒。"或者是"上海的美国领事馆发生了一件事，这使我想起一个极好的故事。"当演讲人以这样的

6.

How to Tell a Story

Someone has wittily said that only those in their anecdotage should tell stories. De Quincey wanted all story-tellers to be submerged in a horse-pond, or treated in the same manner as mad dogs. But story-telling has its legitimate and appropriate use, and if certain rules are observed may give added charm to conversation and public speaking.

It requires a fine discrimination to know when to tell a story, and when not to tell one though it is urging itself to be expressed. Few men have the rare gift of choosing the right story for the particular occasion. Many men have no difficulty in telling stories that are insufferably long, pointless, and uninteresting.

We have all been victims of a certain type of public speaker who begins by saying, "Now I don't want to bore you with a long story, but this is so good, etc.," or "An incident occurred at the American Consulate in Shanghai, which reminds me of an awfully good story, etc." When a speaker prefaces his remarks with some such sentences as

话开场时，我们知道接下来的时间不会好过。

一个好故事应该新颖、优雅、简短、简明、不会冒犯他人，与讲话的话题相配。由于这样的故事很少见，建议大家将发现的好故事记在一个专门的本子上以待不时之需。据说杰出的餐后演讲者昌西·迪普有一个保持了很多年的习惯，就是将在报纸杂志上看到的好故事和其他有趣的资料剪下来贴在本子上。他将剪贴本分门别类地保存着，因此他能够在很短的时间内针对任何一般性的话题为自己的大脑准备好充分的材料。

想要讲故事的人应当清楚记住他要讲的故事，最要命的就是演讲人讲到中间迟疑起来，只好道歉说自己没记清楚，而且说这个故事本来是很好笑的，其实这是在用另一种方式暴露自己的缺点。如果不能流利、生动地讲一个故事，还是应当首先练习一下，试着讲给自己的家人听，当然前提是他们可以耐着性子听下去。

有些故事是需要背诵的，尤其是那些由特定的用语引发幽默效果的故事。在这种情况下，就需要通过一些训练和相应的经验来掩盖背诵过的痕迹。请看下面的故事，很显然，它需要全部背下来：

历史上最长的一次布道花费了三个半小时。而最短的布道是一位传道士只用了一分钟的布

these, we know we are in for an uncomfortable time.

As far as possible a story should be new, clever, short, simple, inoffensive, and appropriate. As such stories are scarce, it is advisable to set them down, when found, in a special note-book for convenient reference. It is said that Chauncey M. Depew, one of the most gifted of after-dinner speakers, was for many years in the habit of keeping a set of scrap-books in which were preserved stories and other interesting data clipped from newspapers and magazines. These were so classified that he could on short notice refresh his mind with ample material upon almost any general subject.

Anyone who essays to tell a story should have it clearly in mind. It is fatal for a speaker to hesitate midway in a story, apologize for not knowing it better, avow that it was much more humorous when told to him, and in other ways to announce his shortcomings. If he cannot tell a story fluently and interestingly, he should first practice it on his own family—provided they will tolerate it.

Some stories should be committed to memory, especially where the point of humor depends upon exact phraseology. In such case, it requires some training and experience to disguise the memorized effort. A story like the following, for obvious reasons, should be thoroughly memorized:

The longest sermon on record occupied three hours and a half. But the shortest sermon was that

道，题目是："人生在世必遇烦恼，正如火星必向上飞。"他说：

"我要将我的演讲分为三个标题：(1)人进入世界(2)人在世上成长(3)人离开世界。

"首先，他赤裸着来到这个世界上。

"然后，烦恼和忧虑伴他在世上成长。

"最后，他离开世界，无人知晓他去了哪里。

"总结一下：

"如果我们在这里生活得很好，那么在其他地方也会一样。

"即使我说上一年，也只能告诉你这些道理。

"好啦，现在开始募捐。"

包含方言的故事通常很难讲，新手最好不要尝试。事实上，没有多少人会讲爱尔兰方言、苏格兰方言、德语方言、伦敦方言以及无需加以夸张的黑人方言。所以在大多数场合，还是用平易的英语讲一些小故事为妙。

讲故事的风格应当是朴实的谈话式的风格。要把注意力集中在所讲的故事上并且真诚地希望将快乐带给听故事的人，这样演讲者才不会感到拘谨。当然讲故事时你不应是首先发笑的人。有时在讲一个幽默故事时，说话人要始终一本正经才

of a preacher who spoke for one minute on the text: "Man is born unto trouble as the sparks fly upward." He said:

"I shall divide my discourse into three heads: (1) Man's ingress into the world; (2) His progress through the world; (3) His egress out of the world.

"Firstly, His ingress into the world is naked and bare.

"Secondly, His progress through the world is trouble and care.

" Thirdly, His egress out of the world is nobody knows where.

"To conclude:

"If we live well here, we shall live well there.

"I can tell you no more if I preach a whole year.

"The collection will now be taken up."

Dialect stories are usually rather difficult, and should not as a general thing be attempted by beginners. As a matter of fact, few persons know how to speak such dialects as Irish, Scotch, German, Cockney, and negro without undue exaggeration. For most occasions it is well to keep to simple stories couched in plain English.

A story should be told in simple, conversational style. Concentration upon the story, and a sincere desire to give pleasure to the hearers, will keep the speaker free from self-consciousness. Needless to say he should not be the first to laugh at his own story. Sometimes in telling a humorous anecdote to an audience a speaker secures the greatest effect by maintaining an expression of

能达到最佳的效果。

无论你多会讲故事，也不要讲太多。一个公认的文采飞扬、风趣幽默的人，若是人们已经听够了，而你还在一个故事接一个故事地一味讲下去的话，也会变得让人厌烦，无法忍受。在所有的演讲者中讲故事的人尤其应当时刻观察他的每一位听众，警觉地捕捉最不显眼的厌烦迹象。

不用说，绝对不应该讲那种可能会冒犯某些人的故事。也许你会博众人一笑，却也会因此失去一个朋友。因此那些有关结巴、红发人、岳母的笑话都应慎重选择。

总的来说，最棒的故事应当妙在最后一刻，幽默的包袱直到结束时才打开。下面这个故事即是如此：

> 一位年老的黑人被带到乡村法官面前。
>
> “杰斯罗，”法官说道，“你被指控偷了约翰逊将军家的鸡，那么你有没有证人？”
>
> “没有啊，老法官大人。”老杰斯罗自豪地回答，“我没有，大人，我从不在证人面前偷鸡。”

阿斯奎斯首相讲的故事和这个类似：

> 英国的一位教授在他的实验室黑板上写道：“布朗克教授通知他的学生们，他今天被

extreme gravity.

No matter how successful one may be in telling stories, he should avoid telling too many. A man who is accounted brilliant and entertaining may become an insufferable bore by continuing to tell stories when the hearers have become satiated. Of all speakers, the story–teller should keep his eyes on his entire audience and be alert to detect the slightest signs of weariness.

It is superfluous to say that a story should never be told which in any way might give offence. The speaker may raise a laugh, but lose a friend. Hence it is that stories about stammerers, red–headed people, mothers–in–law, and the like, should always be chosen with discrimination.

Generally the most effective story is one in which the point of humor is not disclosed until the very last words, as in the following:

An old colored man was brought up before a country judge.

"Jethro," said the judge, "you are accused of stealing General Johnson's chickens. Have you any witnesses?"

"No, sah," old Jethro answered, haughtily; "I hab not,sah. I never steal chickens befo' witnesses."

This is a similar example, told by Prime Minister Asquith:

An English professor wrote on the blackboard in his laboratory, "Professor Blank informs his students that he has this day been appointed

任命为乔治国王的名誉医生。"

上午他有事离开了一会儿，回来时发现一位恶搞的学生在后面添了字："上帝啊，竟然有这种事！"

亨利·格雷迪很会讲故事。举他一个很棒的故事为例：

从前有一个老牧师，一次他提前告诉了圣经课的一些男孩第二天早上他要读哪几段经文，这些男孩便找到那几段经文，把其中的几页粘在了一起。第二天早上当他读到某一页的末尾："当诺亚 120 岁的时候，他给自己娶了个老婆，她"然后他翻到下一页"70 米长，20 米宽，由歌斐木制成，内外都刷上了沥青。"很自然地，他开始感到困惑，于是他又读了一遍，以便确定是否读对了，随后说："我的朋友们，这是我第一次在《圣经》中遇到这段话，但是我认为这说明我们人类的产生是可怕而奇妙的。"

嘲讽和攻击性的性格是十分危险的，但是偶尔善意地打趣却并不坏。举个例子，在一次年末聚餐会上，乔特先生举杯祝酒："为海军干杯。"迪普先生回答道："为陆军干杯。"迪普先生接着讲道："有专业人士在场才便于请教，这就是为什么乔特先生在此向我们提到了海军的原因吧。一次我们在码头上碰见了，但是直到船抵达利物浦我才再

honorary physician to his Majesty, King George."

During the morning he had some occasion to leave the room, and found on his return that some student wag had added the words,

"God save the King!"

Henry W. Grady was a facile story-teller. One of his best stories was as follows:

"There was an old preacher once who told some boys of the Bible lesson he was going to read in the morning. The boys, finding the place, glued together the connecting pages. The next morning he read on the bottom of one page: 'When Noah was one hundred and twenty years old he took unto himself a wife, who was'—then turning the page—'one hundred and forty cubits long, forty cubits wide, built of gopherwood, and covered with pitch inside and out.' He was naturally puzzled at this. He read it again, verified it, and then said: 'My friends, this is the first time I ever met this in the Bible, but I accept it as an evidence of the assertion that we are fearfully and wonderfully made.'"

Personalities based upon sarcasm or invective are always attended with danger, but good-humored bantering may be used upon occasion with most happy results. As an instance of this, there is a story of an annual dinner at which Mr. Choate was set down for the toast, "The Navy," and Mr. Depew was to respond to "The Army." Mr. Depew began by saying, "It's well to have a specialist: that's why Choate is here to speak about the Navy. We met at the wharf once and I did

看到他。我问他感觉如何，他说要是哪怕只是呼吸到了一点点海洋空气，他也会喜欢那次旅行的。好啦，你们肯定想听一听乔特先生对当海军的感受吧。”轮到乔特先生讲话了，他说道：“我听说迪普被认为是最棒的餐后演讲者。如果餐后演讲正如我所听说并且相信的那样，是讲废话的艺术，那么迪普先生则是世界上最最出众的演讲者。”

医生们可以做到虽被抨击却无动于衷，因为他们早已经习惯了。有这么个故事，有一位年轻的工人上班时顺路去了注册部门，想要登记他父亲的死亡。当工作人员问到他父亲的死亡日期时，这位儿子回答道：“他目前还没有死，但是他天黑之前一定会死，所以我想你要是现在帮我登记上的话，就省得我再跑一趟了。”“哦，那可不行。”工作人员说，“也许你的父亲可以活到明天呢。”“噢，不会的，先生；医生说了我父亲不会活到明天，因为他清楚他给了我父亲什么药。”

故事当然是不宜说得太多，但是面对听众，讲一个拿自己开玩笑的故事可能会收到特别好的效果。比如：

> 上一次作过演讲后，第二天我就去拜访了本地一家报社的主编。我说：
>
> “贵报过去可是支持我的，对不对？”
>
> 主编说：“是啊，怎么了？”
>
> “很好，”我说，“我昨晚作了个演讲，可

not see him again till we reached Liverpool. When I asked how he felt he said he thought he would have enjoyed the trip over if he had had any ocean air. Yes, you want to hear Choate on the Navy." When it was Mr. Choate's turn to speak, he said: "I've heard Depew hailed as the greatest after-dinner speaker. If after-dinner speaking, as I have heard it described and as I believe it to be, is the art of saying nothing at all, then Mr. Depew is the most marvelous speaker in the universe."

The medical profession can be assailed with impunity, since they have long since grown accustomed to it. There is a story of a young laborer who, on his way to his day's work, called at the registrar's office to register his father's death. When the official asked the date of the event, the son replied, "He ain't dead yet, but he'll be dead before night, so I thought it would save me another journey if you would put it down now." "Oh, that won't do at all," said the registrar; "perhaps your father will live till tomorrow." "Well, I don't think so, sir; the doctor says as he won't, and he knows what he has given him."

While stories should be used sparingly, there is probably nothing more effective before a popular audience than the telling of a story in which the joke is on the speaker himself. Thus:

The last time I made a speech, I went next day to the editor of our local newspaper, and said,

"I thought your paper was friendly to me?"

The editor said, "So it is. What's the matter?"

"Well," I said, "I made a speech last night, and

是，今天早晨你们的报纸上却对我的演讲只字未提。”

“没错。”主编说，“这不恰恰证明我们对您很宽容吗。”

许多效果非常好的精彩故事本身都很严肃。这里有一个曾被成功地使用过的故事：一些西部来的先生们议论起政府的职责与过失时既兴奋，又忧虑重重。林肯总统耐心地听完他们的话，然后回答道：“先生们，假设你们所有的财产是一大笔黄金，而你将其交给走索道的人靠一根绳索穿越尼亚加拉河。那么你会不会摇动绳索，或者不断地冲他喊：‘嘿，站直点；嘿，弯点腰。走快点，往北挪点，往南挪点。’不，你不会。你会屏住呼吸，闭上嘴，把手拿开，直到他安全上岸。我们的政府肩负着巨大的压力，我们的手中是人民的巨万财富。我们正竭尽全力做自己的工作。不要打扰我们，保持安静，这样我们才能顺利地抵达对岸。”

双关语显然已经过时了。最巧妙的英语双关来自汤姆·胡德：

“他去将秘密告诉了敲钟人，

而敲钟人去教堂敲响了钟。”

（“told”——“告诉”与 tolled——“敲响”同音异义，构成双关语。 ——译者注）

约翰逊博士说双关语是最低层次的幽默。但是，有的时候那些异常睿智、自然贴切的双关语也会给人带来美的享受。例如：

you didn't print a single line of it this morning."

"Well," said the editor, "what further proof do you want?"

Many of the best and most effective stories are serious in character. One that has been used successfully is this: Some gentlemen from the West were excited and troubled about the commissions or omissions of the administration. President Lincoln heard them patiently, and then replied:"Gentlemen, suppose all the property you were worth was in gold, and you had put it in the hands of Blondin to carry across the Niagara River on a rope; would you shake the cable, or keep shouting out to him—'Blondin, stand up a little straighter—Blondin, stoop a little more—go a little faster—lean a little more to the north—lean a little more to the south?' No, you would hold your breath as well as your tongue, and keep your hands off until he was safe over. The Government is carrying an immense weight. Untold treasures are in our hands. We are doing the very best we can. Don't badger us. Keep silence, and we'll get you safe across."

Punning is of course out of fashion. The best pun in the English language is Tom Hood's:

"He went and told the sexton,
And the sexton tolled the bell."

Dr. Johnson said that the pun was the lowest order of wit. But punning, when it is unusually clever and spontaneous, may be thoroughly enjoyable, as in the following:

最高法院首席法官斯托里出席了波士顿的一个晚餐会，席间爱德华·埃弗雷特也在场。博学的首席法官想要赞誉一下埃弗雷特，于是便主动举杯祝酒：

“埃弗雷特处处留政绩，口碑载道。”

才华横溢的学者也站起来回应道：

“这个国家的司法学问再高，也高不过一层楼的高度（“story”——既可作一层楼讲，也指斯托里的姓名——“Story”　——译者注）。”

对于有超强记忆力和丰富词汇量的人而言，讲故事这种形式可能会弄巧成拙。然而，所谓的机智应答这种幽默形式就应该慎用或是在有可能成为冒犯的情况下禁用。

在这方面博·布鲁梅尔是惭愧的。有一次一位女士问他要不要喝杯茶时，他俏皮地说：“谢谢，除了药我什么都不喝。”女主人答道：“真不好意思，不过你说话倒是挺不见外的嘛。”

有个关于亨利·勒特雷尔的故事。他在爱尔兰议会任职多年，但是没有人知道他的确切年龄。有一天，霍兰夫人毫不顾及礼貌，直截了当地问道：“我们都太想知道您的年龄了，请告诉我吧。”勒特雷尔严肃地回答道：“这是个古怪的问题，但是既然您霍兰夫人提出来了，我并不介意告诉您，如果我能活到明年，我就老得成精了！”

并没有什么学校传授讲故事的艺术，因此只有为数不多的人能够在不违反从经验得出的规则

Chief Justice Story attended a public dinner in Boston at which Edward Everett was present. Desiring to pay a delicate compliment to the latter, the learned judge proposed as a volunteer toast:

"Fame follows merit where Everett goes."

The brilliant scholar arose and responded:

" To whatever heights judicial learning may attain in this country, it will never get above one Story."

Story-telling may attain the character of a disease, in one who has a retentive memory and a voluble vocabulary. The form of humor known as repartee, however, is one that requires rare discrimination. It should be used sparingly, and not at all if it is likely to give offence.

Beau Brummell was guilty in this respect, when he was once asked by a lady if he would"take a cup of tea." "Thank you," said he, "I never *take* anything but physic." "I beg your pardon," said the hostess, "you also take liberties."

There is a story that Henry Luttrell had sat long in the Irish Parliament, but no one knew his precise age. Lady Holland, without regard to considerations of courtesy, one day said to him point-blank, "Now, we are all dying to know how old you are. Just tell me." Luttrell answered very gravely, "It is an odd question, but as you, Lady Holland, ask it, I don´t mind telling you. If I live till next year, I shall be—devilish old!"

The art of story-telling is not taught specifically, hence there are comparatively few people who can tell a story without violating some

的前提下把故事讲好。但是应该鼓励人们把故事作为谈话的点缀和精彩演说的有用辅助手段加以合理利用。如果肯在我们的建议上下些功夫的话，许多人会成为讲故事的高手。它并不是一门高深的艺术，但是就像其他科目一样也需要研究与运用。

在讲故事方面给演说者的最好的忠告如下：对要讲述的故事了如指掌；事先把故事讲给某人以测试其效果;对它进行适当的修改以适应特殊的场合;故事要简洁,省略不必要的枝节性的东西；准备比计划更多的故事，因为如果你是名单上最后一个演讲者，那么轮到你的时候你所准备的最精彩的故事或许已经被前面的演讲者讲过了。最后,当你已经成功时,要懂得见好就收。

of the rules which experience recommends. But the right use of story-telling should be encouraged as an ornament of conversation, and a valuable auxiliary to effective public address. Many people might excel as story-tellers if they would devote a little time to suggestions such as are offered here. It is not a difficult art, but like every other subject requires study and application.

The best counsel for public speakers in the matter of story-telling may be summed up as follows: Know your story thoroughly; test your story by telling it to some one in advance; adapt your story to the special circumstances; be concise, omitting non-essentials; have ready more stories than you intend to use, because if you should speak at the end of the list you may find that your best story has been told by a previous speaker; and, finally, always stop when you have made a hit.

7.

推销中的谈话技巧

推销员的成功与否主要取决于交谈能力。当然他所推销的产品必须有其真正的优点，并且他必须对所推销的产品有全面的了解。但是为了使其努力取得最佳的效果，他必须知道怎样进行有效的交谈。

适用于成功交谈的一切普遍要求也同样适用于推销员。他应具有悦耳的嗓音、温和的态度、一套恰到好处的实用的词汇以及把事情说清楚并让人信服的能力。

莫与顾客争论是推销员的黄金法则。他可以解释、说理，可以调动他掌握的所有有说服力的措辞，但他绝不能允许自己与顾客争论。因为争论对于成功的推销是致命的障碍。

对于推销员，招人喜欢的个性是无可取代的。这样的个性是由哪些要素构成的呢？简单地说就是好听的嗓音、亲切的态度、坦率的话语，落落大

7.

Talking in Salesmanship

The salesman depends for his success primarily upon his talking ability. Obviously, what he offers for sale must have intrinsic merit, and he should possess a thorough knowledge of his wares. But in order to secure the best results from his efforts, he must know how to talk well.

All the general requirements for good conversation apply equally to the needs of the salesman. He should have a pleasant speaking voice and an agreeable manner, a vocabulary of useful and appropriate words, and the ability to put things clearly and convincingly.

It should be a golden rule of the salesman never to argue with the customer. He may explain and reason, and use all the persuasive phraseology at his command, but he must not permit himself for a single instant to engage in controversy. To argue is fatal to successful salesmanship.

There is nothing that can be substituted for a winning personality in the salesman. What constitutes such a personality? Chiefly a good voice, affability of manner, straightforward speech, manly

方的风度、殷勤待人的拳拳诚心、得体的穿着和良好的个人卫生习惯。以上这些是任何渴望在推销方面成功的人都能做到的。

几乎所有推销员都会碰到一些意料之外的问题，比如，敏感或易怒的顾客可能会莫名其妙地生气或感到未受尊重。这时推销员该怎么做？他应该特别注意不要流露出丝毫的厌恶。反驳顾客或是与其争吵可是推销员担当不起的，即使他是完全无辜的。一旦他开口，便应该平心静气、通情达理，任何时候都不要忘记谈话的目的——说服顾客接受对你有利的观点。

成功的推销员必须有一定的策略和辨别力。他必须知晓什么时候怎样避免一些就要脱口而出的、最终往往会被证明是不明智的言辞。他必须训练自己在困境中迅速地选择一条正确的、最佳的谈话途径。

推销员应该专心致志地与顾客打交道。讲话的时候必须表达得清晰直接、简洁易懂。听对方讲话时则应饶有兴趣地倾听，不能走神，对方的话要声声入耳。

推销员应知道何时讲话、何时保持沉默。有的顾客希望你告诉他较多的信息，有的则更愿意自己思考。聪明的推销员知道何时该缄口不语，过于

bearing, the desire to serve and please, proper attire, and cleanliness of person. These qualifications come within the reach of anyone who aspires to success in salesmanship.

Every salesman has unexpected problems to solve. A sensitive or touchy customer may become unreasonably angry or offended. What is the salesman to do? He should here be particularly on his guard not to show the slightest resentment. Though he may be wholly guiltless, he cannot afford to contradict the customer, nor to challenge him to a vocal duel. If he talks at all, he should talk quietly and reasonably, and always with the object of bringing the customer around to a favorable point of view.

The successful salesman must have tact and discrimination. He must know when and how to check in himself the word or phrase which is trying to force its way out into expression, but which would in the end prove inadvisable. He must train himself to choose quickly the right and best course under difficult circumstances.

The salesman should give his undivided attention to the customer. If the salesman is speaking, he should speak clearly, directly, concisely, and understandingly; if he is listening, he should listen interestedly and thoroughly, with all his powers alive and receptive.

The salesman should know when to speak and when to be silent. Some customers wish to be told much, others prefer to think for themselves. He is a wise salesman who knows when to be mute.

话多往往会适得其反地毁掉良好的推销机会。

推销员应把握一种合适的语调。语调不宜高也不宜低，应该听起来悦耳并足以抓住潜在购买者的注意力。每个推销员都应该培养有乐感的、音量适中的嗓音并将其作为推销术的主要资本。

推销员应该培养优雅的谈吐和端庄的举止，人们一般厌恶过分亲昵、乱开玩笑和任意胡闹。最好先姑且认定顾客是严肃的，他所说的并非妄语也不想跟你逗着玩。不用说，在推销的过程中，讲冗长的故事或是个人经历更是不可取的。

讲述短小的故事也有其合适的时间和地点。跟其他一切事物一样，讲故事也要有适宜的环境才有好的效果。林肯就很善于利用讲故事的手段，但他曾经说过："很多人都知道我爱讲故事，但我并不是通常意义上爱讲故事的人。因为吸引我的并不是故事本身，而是讲故事的目的和效果。我经常用可以阐明我观点的小故事来避开别人冗长无用的辩论或是省去自己的费力解释。"

在任何情况下，推销员都绝不能失去沉着和风度。动辄怒气冲冲绝不可能招来生意。在适当的

Loquacity has often killed what otherwise might have been a good sale.

There is a certain tone of voice which the salesman should aim to acquire. It is neither high nor low in pitch. It is agreeable to the listening ear, and is almost sufficient in itself to win the favorable attention of the prospective buyer. Every salesman should cultivate a musical and well-modulated voice as one of the chief assets in salesmanship.

The salesman should cultivate dignity of speech and manner. People generally dislike familiarity, joking, and horse-play. It is well to assume that the customer is serious-minded, that he means business and nothing else. Needless to say, the telling of long stories, or personal experiences, has no legitimate place in the business of salesmanship.

There is a proper time and place for short story-telling. Like everything else it is all right in its appropriate setting. Lincoln used it to advantage, but once said: "I believe I have the popular reputation of being a story-teller, but I do not deserve the name in its general sense; for it is not the story itself, but its purpose, or effect, that interests me. I often avoid a long and useless discussion by others, or a laborious explanation on my part, by a short story that illustrates my point of view."

The salesman should resolve not to lose his poise and agreeableness under any circumstances. Irritability never attracts business. To say the right

场合说适当的话是最理想的，但同样重要且更难能可贵的是在心旌摇荡的时候仍能做到自我克制不说错话。

对于推销员而言，强迫顾客购买其并不需要的商品是不正当的，但是顾客往往并不清楚自己要的是什么也不知道什么东西是可以派上用场的。因此称职的推销员应当知晓怎样运用一切正当的方式来影响顾客做出有利于自己的决定。

顾客的推托之词并不一定就是定局。他或许并不十分清楚你所提供的产品的优点或用途。也许他需要推销员的解释或建议以便得出正确的结论,这正是推销员可以发挥最重要作用的时刻。

依靠自己与狂妄自大截然不同，每个人都应充分地自信,这在各行各业都是必要的。但是,对于推销员来说,这一点远比绝大多数人都更重要,他必须格外地相信自己和所出售的产品。

然而,这种自信绝不等同于冒失或自负。礼貌和周到是优秀推销员必备的首要素质。反之,自吹自擂、油嘴滑舌、自私自利、大喊大叫和强词夺理既不可取又令人反感。

沉默所具有的雄辩力和说服力在推销的艺术

thing in the right place is desirable, but it is quite as important, though more difficult, to leave unsaid the wrong thing at the moment of temptation.

It is not the legitimate business of the salesman to force upon a customer what is really not wanted, but many times the customer does not know what he wants nor what he might be able to use. Hence the competent salesman should know how to influence the customer towards a favorable decision, using all honorable and approved means to bring about such a result.

The customer's unfavorable answer is not to be accepted always as final. He may not clearly understand the merits or uses of the article offered. He may need the explanations and suggestions of the salesman in order to reach a right conclusion. Here it is that the salesman may fulfill one of his most important duties.

There is a wide difference between self-reliance and obtrusiveness. Every man should have a full degree of self-confidence. It is needed in every walk in life. But the salesman, more than most men, must have an exceptional degree of faith in himself and in what he has to sell.

This self-confidence, however, is a very different thing from boldness or obtrusiveness. Courtesy and considerateness are cardinal qualities of the well-equipped salesman, but boastfulness, glibness, egotism, loudness, and self-assertion, are as distasteful as they are undesirable.

The eloquence and persuasiveness of silence is nowhere better exemplified than in the art of

中得到了最好的证明。说得多的人卖的少，而说的少的人却卖得多。二者中的胜出者成功的原因主要在于他很清楚如何介绍所售产品的优点、怎样把话说得简洁而有效、怎样通过自己的人格魅力赢得顾客的好感，还知道何时应该停止讲话。

现代的推销主要以准确的判断力为基础。一个有头脑的人或许会轻易地胜过比他更有经验的推销员，即使他可能在其他条件上有所欠缺。对于任何人来讲，能够准确思考、深入推理、迅速衡量情况都是难能可贵的。

无论何时，推销员都应该说话得体有礼。如果一个推销员有两套谈话标准，特殊场合使用较高标准，而其他场合用较低标准，这是不明智的。他应有意识地在声调、发音、表达和言辞方面培养自己，以期形成一种日常习惯。这不仅仅是推销员应该不断追求的目标，也应该是每个渴望成功、渴望有所建树的人的共同目标。

salesmanship. One man says much, and sells little; another says little, and sells much. The reason for the superior success of one over the other is mainly due to the fact that he knows best how to present the merits of what he offers for sale, knows how to say it concisely and effectively, knows how to ingratiate himself, largely through his personality, into the good graces of the prospective buyer, and knows when to stop talking.

Modern salesmanship is based primarily upon common sense. A man with brains, though possibly lacking in other desirable qualifications, may easily outdistance the more experienced salesman. It is a valuable thing in any man to be able to think accurately, reason deeply, and size up a situation promptly.

The salesman should at all times be on his best talking behavior. It is not advisable for him to have two standards of speech, and to use an inferior one excepting for special occasions. He should cultivate as a regular daily habit discrimination in the use of voice, enunciation, expression, and language. This should be the constant aim not only of the salesman, but of every man ambitious to achieve success and distinction in the world.

8.

谈话者及其癖好

有个故事讲的是一位政治家面对听众讲话时习惯用手摸衣服上的一个纽扣。有一次，一位朋友偷偷地剪下了那枚纽扣，结果当他站起来发言时，就找不到演讲的思路了。

格拉德斯通讲话时习惯用握紧的右拳击打左手手掌，因此需要特殊强调的词常常被击打的声音遮盖。杰出的政治家有一个共同的习惯：将右手高高举起，然后肘部弯曲，用拇指的指甲轻轻地搔抓头顶。

鲍尔弗在讲话时常常用双手揪住其西服胸前的翻领，那样子就好像生怕自己在把话讲完之前逃走。

戈申在刚开始讲话时总要用手指触探胸部和肋部，确信肋骨状况正常之后，便会像用肥皂洗手

8.

Men and Mannerisms

There is a story of a politician who had acquired a mannerism of fingering a button on his coat while talking to an audience. On one occasion some friends surreptitiously cut the particular button off, and the result was that the speaker when he stood up to address the audience lost the thread of his discourse.

Gladstone had a mannerism of striking the palm of his left hand with the clenched fist of his other hand, so that often the emphatic word was lost in the noise of percussion. A common habit of the distinguished statesman was to reach out his right hand at full arm's length, and then to bend it back at the elbow and lightly scratch the top of his head with his thumb-nail.

Balfour, while speaking, used to take hold of the lapels of his coat by both hands as if he were in mortal fear of running away before he had finished.

Goshen, at the beginning of a speech, would sound his chest and sides with his hands, and apparently finding that his ribs were in good order,

似的搓弄双手。

但奇怪的是讲话者往往意识不到自己讲话时的怪癖，而且常常率先指责他人讲话时的特殊习惯。克服这种缺点的方法是彻底而严格地自责自律。一个有着令人反感的讲话习惯的演讲家纵然很出众，也只有在克服了这些小毛病之后才会更加优秀。

每一个演说家都有与他人不同的声音和举止上的特点。如果这种特点能使演说风格更加生动有效，它便是可取的，应该给予鼓励。但是当这种特点显得很怪或者在某种意义上会使人不快时，那它便属于纯粹的怪癖，应予以纠正。

一种令人反感的声调习惯被称为“传教调”，它和某些“传教士”布道的习惯声调有关。“传教调”有好几种形式，例如，过高地拔高声调、拖得很长的声调、从声调的一个极端到另一个极端的突然转变，或是屈尊俯就的语气。还有一种是鲜有抑扬变化、听起来悲悲切切的声调，这种声调使讲话风格显得甚是哀伤。这些都偏离了高水准传教所应有的自然、认真、真诚和直接的布道风格。

此外还有一个令人厌恶的语调癖好，即在几个语义表达完整的句子之后上扬语调。这样做会

would proceed to wash his hands with invisible soap.

The strange thing about mannerisms is that the speakers are usually unconscious of them, and would be the first to condemn them in others. The remedy for such defects lies in thorough and severe self-examination and self-criticism. However eminent a speaker may be with objectionable mannerisms, he would be still greater without them.

Every public speaker has certain characteristics of voice and manner that distinguish him from other men. In so far as this individuality gives increased power and effectiveness to the speaking style, it is desirable and should be encouraged. When, however, it is carried to excess, or in any sense offends good taste, it is merely mannerism, and should be discouraged.

There is an objectionable mannerism of the voice, known as "pulpit tone," that has come to be associated with some preachers. It takes various forms, such as an unduly elevated key, a drawling monotone, a sudden transition from one extreme of pitch to another, or a tone of condescension. It is also heard in a plaintive minor inflection, imparting a quality of extreme sadness to a speaker's style. These are all departures from the natural, earnest, sincere, and direct delivery that belongs to the high office of preaching.

Still another undesirable mannerism of the voice is that of giving a rising inflection at the close of successive sentences that are obviously

让演讲者的思绪悬在半空，而听众则感到失望或是疑虑,几个句子的意义很可能被完全误解。除非显然需要语调上扬转折，否则用这种方式表达的观点则缺乏重点和力度,不具说服力。

装模作样、矫揉造作、浮夸卖弄、言过其实、信口开河、过度热情、单调乏味、拖腔拿调及一切有损简洁、热诚的缺点都应该避免。过多的强调会使讲话人的观点显得过激。若演讲者带着一定要做一次“了不起的演讲”的思想负担或许会使演讲者在整个演讲过程中焦躁不安。

清晰准确的吐字发音是必要的，但不能刻意卖弄，不应让听众的注意力被吸引到你的吐字发音上去。“你的表演让我忘了听你在说什么。”——这句话也同样适用于演讲者的举止。嘴形夸张、嘴唇发出叭咂声、过分重读词尾辅音、拖长齿擦音的嘶嘶声,这些都是应该受到谴责的做法。犹豫不决、在较难的词语连接处结结巴巴、词尾音节发得含糊不清、把一个词的尾音同下一个词的首音合在一起等等，都是训练有素的演讲者不能被原谅的错误。

同样的抑扬语调重复过多也就成了一种怪僻——千篇一律的变化模式。这让我们想起了只奏一个曲调的手摇风琴,总之,反复地听同一个调子是一种痛苦。对于一个公众人物而言,这样的演

complete. Here the speaker's thought is left suspended in the air, the hearer feels a sense of disappointment or doubt, and possibly the entire meaning is perverted. Thoughts delivered in such a manner, unless they distinctly require a rising inflection, lack the emphasis and force of persuasive speaking.

Artificiality, affectation, pomposity, mouthing, undue vehemence, monotony, intoning, and everything that detracts from the simplicity and genuine fervor of the speech should be avoided. Too much emphasis may drive a thought beyond the mark, and a conscious determination to make a "great speech" may keep the speaker in a state of anxiety throughout its entire delivery.

A clear and correct enunciation is essential, but it should not be pedantic, nor should it attract attention to itself. "What you are prevents me from hearing what you say," might also be applied to the manner of the speaker. Exaggerated opening of the mouth, audible smacking of the lips, holding tenaciously to final consonants, prolonged hissing of sibilants, are all to be condemned. Hesitation, stumbling over difficult combinations, obscuring final syllables, coalescing the last sound of one word with the first sound of the following word, are inexcusable in a trained speaker.

When the same modulation of the voice is repeated too often, it becomes a mannerism, a kind of monotony of variety. It reminds one of a street-piano set to but one tune, and is quite as distressing to a sensitive ear. This is not the style

讲方式并不符合人们的期望。

那么演讲者在演讲的时候应该用手做些什么呢？除非特别需要把某个想法表达得更加完整，否则实际上什么都不用做。让手臂放松地自然垂在身体的两侧，以备即刻可用。演讲者将拳头抵在背部的腰眼上来“支撑”身体、紧揪着外套的翻领、拍击双手发出声响、“粗俗随意”地把双手放在臀部、把手插在裤子口袋里、像“用肥皂洗手似的”搓弄双手或是突然用力捶打讲台等，都属于令人生厌的怪癖。

在演讲刚开始时把手置于背后也许会显得神态轻松，但这种姿势过于僵硬、缺乏活力，不应长时间地保持。将手臂交叉着俯在讲台上等于暂时弃之不用。散漫慵懒地斜倚着讲台、屈膝及其他无精打采的姿态是安闲的歇息姿态，若出现在一个试图说服别人的清醒的演讲者身上则是极为不合适的。

来回摇晃身体、突然翘起脚尖以示强调、低头弯腰、用力跺脚、不时地跳来跳去、表演的成分太多或者刻意模仿他人以及各种各样的激烈或出格的动作在演讲中都最好避免。要当心别走极端。既不要像雕像似的一动不动，也不能不停地手舞足蹈。渴望得到尊严本身是无可厚非的，但我们不要

that is expected from a public man.

What should the speaker do with his hands? Do nothing with them unless they are specifically needed for the more complete expression of a thought. Let them drop at the sides in their natural relaxed position, ready for instant use. To press the fist in the hollow of the back in order to "support" the speaker, to clutch the lapels of the coat, to slap the hands audibly together, to place the hands on the hips in the attitude of "vulgar ease," to put the hands into the pockets, to wring the hands as if "washing them with invisible soap," or to violently pound the pulpit—these belong to the list of undesirable mannerisms.

At the beginning of a speech it may give the appearance of ease to place the hands behind the back, but this position lacks force and action and should not be long sustained. To cross the arms upon the desk is to put them out of commission for the time being. Leaning or lounging of any kind, bending at the knee, or other evidence of weakness or weariness, may belong to the repose of the easy chair, but are hardly appropriate in a wide-awake speaker seeking to convince men.

Rocking the body to and fro, rising on the toes to emphasize, crouching, stamping the foot, springing from side to side, over-acting and impersonation, and violence and extravagance of every description may well be omitted in public speaking. Beware of extremes. Avoid a statue-like attitude on the one hand and a constant restlessness on the other. Dignity is desirable, but one should not

忘记萨姆·琼斯牧师的话“没有什么比死尸更有尊严。”

过于频繁的相同手势很快便会失去其应有的分量。如果使用手势，也应将手势做得完整而富有变化以示轻松和随意。若只做一半，则很有可能让人莫名其妙，这不但不能帮你表明观点反而会让你的观点难于理解。频频的手势会让人眼花缭乱，给人以不够沉着镇定的印象。

年轻的演讲者应尤其注意不要模仿他人的演讲风格，因为对某人而言极其自然的风格用在另一个人身上也许是非常可笑的。卡迪纳尔·纽曼讲话时极其谨慎，每个音节都要小心翼翼地发得准确;而菲利普·布鲁克斯讲话则如子弹连发，一分钟能说出二百多个单词。然而一般的演讲者要仿效这些例子的话可就危险了。

还有一种类型的演讲也可谓别具一格。它的独特性虽然从严格意义上讲并不是怪癖，却也不利于获得演讲的最佳效果。其表现是有气无力，演讲者的样子始终都疲惫不堪，其演讲听起来似乎是在敷衍了事。他的声音和举止毫无生气，这也影响到了听众，因此他的话不可能给听众留下深刻而长久的印象。约瑟夫·帕克曾说过当星期日到来时，他感觉自己就像一匹蓄势待发的赛马，迫不及待地想要赶去教堂的讲坛发表演讲。

forget the words of the Reverend Sam Jones,"There is nothing more dignified than a corpse!"

Gestures that are too frequent and alike soon lose their significance. If they are attempted at all they should be varied and complete, suggesting freedom and spontaneity. When only half made they are likely to call attention to the discrepancy, and to this extent will obscure rather than help the thought. The continuous use of gesture is displeasing to the eye, and gives the impression of lack of poise.

The young speaker particularly should be warned not to imitate the speaking style of others. What is perfectly natural to one may appear ridiculous in another. Cardinal Newman spoke with extreme deliberateness, enunciating every syllable with care and precision; Phillips Brooks sent forth an avalanche of words at the rate of two hundred a minute; but it would be dangerous for the average speaker to emulate either of these examples.

There is a peculiarity in a certain type of speaking, which, while not strictly a mannerism, is detrimental to the highest effect. It manifests itself in physical weakness. The speaker is uniformly tired, and his speaking has a half-hearted tone. The lifelessness in voice and manner communicates itself to the audience, and prevents all possibility of deep and enduring impression. Joseph Parker said that when Sunday came he felt like a racehorse, and could hardly wait for the time to come for him to go into the pulpit. He longed to speak.

训练有素的演讲家在说话的声音和外表上都显得很有修养。表达所需的一切手段都要听从他的指挥，而他则要确保这些手段自然且及时地完成任务。演讲的时候他应该对他的话题全神贯注，应该相信在悉心练习之后他的发言会自行达到预期效果。

The well—equipped speaker is one who has a superior culture of voice and body. All the instruments of expression must be made his obedient servants, but as master of them he should see to it that they perform their work naturally and spontaneously. He should be able while speaking to abandon himself wholly to his subject, confident that as a result of conscientious training his delivery may be left largely to take care of itself.

9.

怎样做好演讲

一次成功的演讲包括两个基本条件：

首先，要做到言之有物。

其次，要掌握表达的技巧。

第一个条件暗含着明智的选题以及最充分的准备。这意味着演讲者已仔细地将可利用的最有参考价值的材料收集到一起，并且比听众中的任何人都更熟悉演讲的话题。

许多演讲者都未能达到准备充分这一要求。由于没有意识到这项艰苦的第一步工作的重要性，他们往往只是站在台上传达给听众极为有限的有价值信息。华丽的修辞、长词的堆砌难以掩饰他们思想的贫乏，因此严肃认真的人也不会信服他们。

同时，我想提醒大家的是，“言之有物”并不

9.

How to Speak in Public

There are two essential qualifications for making an effective public speech.

First, having something worth-while to say.

Second, knowing how to say it.

The first qualification implies a judicious choice of subject and the most thorough preparation. It means that the speaker has carefully gathered together the best available material, and has so familiarized himself with his subject that he knows more about it than anyone else in his audience.

It is in this requirement of thorough preparation that many public speakers are deficient. They do not realize the need for this painstaking preliminary work, and hence they frequently stand before an audience with little information of value to impart to their hearers. Their poverty of thought can not be long disguised in flamboyant rhetoric and sesquipedalian words, and hence they fail to carry conviction to serious-minded men.

I would remind you that having something worth-while to say involves more than thorough

仅仅包括演讲者对特定话题的充分准备，而且演讲者还应确有真才实学。大家都有过这样的经历，在聆听某位演讲者的演讲时，深深吸引我们的不仅仅是他所讲的话题，同时还有他的人格魅力。正是他的人格魅力和厚积薄发的学问令你折服。

通常来讲，使人信服的是演讲者的内在素养而非他嘴上所表达的东西。正如你听一个人讲话，你认为他是值得信赖的，实则因为他凭借的是丰富的阅历和渊博的知识。他的话语源于他的真才实学。

因此，从广义上讲，素养是非常重要的，这种素养包括良好的判断力、权衡轻重缓急的意识、大量的有价值的观点、事实、理由、例证以及丰富的见识。

每一个希望在公众场合发表演说的人都应培养自己的判断能力，或者说养成判断事实或理由真伪的习惯。这样的人会摒弃偏见并不惜一切地探求真相，他不会把真伪人为地强加于客观事物，而是只从事实出发辨别真伪。

在各类书刊迅猛增加的今天，五花八门的出版物争夺着我们的时间和精力。因此在对书籍的选择上，我们应培养敏锐的鉴别力，这一点特别必

preparation of the particular subject which the speaker is to present to an audience. The speaker should have a well–furnished mind. You have had the experience of listening to a public speaker who commanded your closest attention not only because of what he said, but also because of what he was. He inspired confidence in you because of his personality and reserve power.

It is often what a man has within himself, rather than what he actually expresses, that carries greatest conviction to your mind. As you listen to such a man speak, you feel that he is worthy of your confidence because he draws upon broad experience and knowledge. He speaks out of the fulness of a well–furnished mind.

It is important, therefore, that there should be mental culture in a broad way,—sound judgment, a sense of proportion and perspective, a fund of useful ideas, facts, arguments, and illustrations, and a large stock of common sense.

Every man who essays to speak in public should cultivate a judicial mind, or the habit of weighing and estimating facts and arguments. Such a mind is supposedly free from prejudice and seeks the truth at any cost. Such a mind does not want this or that to be necessarily true, but wants to recognize as true only that which is true.

In these days of multiplied publications and books of all kinds, when printed matter of every description is soliciting our time and attention, it is particularly desirable that we should cultivate a discriminating taste in our choice of books. The

要。阅读的最终目的是获得有用的知识与提高个人修养,我们要时刻把这两个目标放在心上。值得注意的是那些在世界上取得不朽业绩的人手边总会有一本好书供其翻阅。

如果你曾在书籍的选择上犹豫不决，你可以向从事文学工作的朋友或向当地图书馆的工作人员寻求帮助。但无论何时,都应抵制那种毫无意义并不能充实头脑的书籍或出版物。

如果你读的书属于自己所有那是最好不过的了。这种个人所有的意识将给你的阅读带来兴趣和快乐,而读不属于自己的书则没有这种效果。同时更为重要的是，你可以用铅笔在自己的书上随意地做标记以便日后的参考。此外,最好准备一个笔记本,在想到有价值的观点时可以随时记下来。

接下来我们谈一下笔的用途。从习惯于写下自己的所思所想这个意义上说，世界上所有的著名演说家都可算做是多产的作家。这也是理清思路、事先检验口头表达以避免谬误的唯一方法。演讲家应多多动笔以便形成一种流畅的、条理清晰的英语运用风格。令人惊奇的是,许多在我们自己看来既清晰又理想的观点一旦想动笔确切地写下来时却变得模糊不清了。

highest purpose of reading is for the acquisition of useful knowledge and personal culture, and we should keep these two aims constantly before us. It is noteworthy that men who have achieved enduring greatness in the world have always had a good book at their ready command.

If you are ever in doubt about the choice of books, you would do well to enlist the services of a literary friend, or ask the advice of a local librarian. But in any case, be on your guard against books and other publications of commonplace type, which can contribute nothing to the enrichment of your mind and life.

It is desirable that you should own the books you read. The sense of personal possession will give an interest and pleasure to your reading which it would not otherwise have, and moreover you can freely mark such books with your pencil for subsequent reference. It is also well to have a note-book conveniently ready in which to jot down useful ideas as they occur to you.

Here we come to the use of the pen. All the great orators of the world have been prolific writers in the sense of writing out their thoughts. It is the only certain way to clarify your thought, to test it in advance of verbal expression and to examine it critically. The public speaker should write much in order to form a clear and flowing English style. It is surprising how many of our thoughts which appear to us clear and satisfactory, assume a peculiar vagueness when we attempt to set them down definitely in writing.

笔的运用常常使演讲者的演讲风格变得思路清晰、语言简洁，让演讲者本人变得谨慎并追求准确。同时，也有助于加深演讲的观点在其头脑中的印象，从而使这些观点在发表演说时可以召之即来。

一个知识完备的大脑就像一幢陈设齐全的房子。在布置房子时，我们并不是把各式各样的家具、小饰物以及古玩等杂乱无章地堆放在一起，而是从和谐、美观、实用的角度做好规划。我们布置某个房间时也会力求让房间的主人感到舒适惬意。在着眼于整体效果的前提下，我们带着明确的目的去挑选每一件家具、地毯、图片以及帷帘等物品。

一个知识完备的头脑也是如此，然而我们必须对打算存在脑中的材料进行选择。选择时需着眼于其美的价值、功效以及实用性。大脑所需要的是可利用的最有价值的材料而不是垃圾。因此为了完善自己的头脑，我们要将世界上的伟大著作、尚在世的权威人士、大自然、音乐、艺术等一切可找到的美好事物作为资料的正确来源，这一点至关重要。

成功演说的第二个根本要素是清楚如何表述，这一点意味着我们要对演讲的技巧进行全面的训练。演讲者的嗓音要好听，其音量要适中、其音质要丰满而有磁性。除此之外，还应在表达、发

The use of the pen tends to give clearness and conciseness to the speaker's style. It makes him careful and accurate. It aids, too, in fixing the ideas of his speech in his mind, so that at the moment of addressing an audience they will respond most readily to his needs.

A well-furnished mind is like a well-furnished house. In furnishing a house we do not fill it up with miscellaneous furniture, bric-a-brac and antiques, gathered promiscuously, but we plan everything with a view to harmony, beauty, and utility. We furnish a particular room in a tone that will be restful and pleasing to the occupant. We choose every piece of furniture, rug, picture, and drapery with a distinct purpose in view of what the total effect will be.

So with a well-furnished mind. We must choose the kind of material we intend to keep there. It should be chosen with a view to its beauty, power, and usefulness. We want no rubbish there. We want the best material available. Hence the vital importance of going to the right sources for the furniture of our mind, to the great books of the world, to living authorities, to nature, to music, to art, to the best wherever it may be found.

The second essential of an effective public speech is knowing how to say it. This implies a thorough training in the technique of speech. There should be a well-cultivated voice, of adequate volume, brilliancy, and carrying quality. There should be ample training in articulation,

音、表情以及手势等方面进行充分的训练。这些所谓的技巧都要不断地锻炼直到它们自然地成为演讲者演讲风格的一部分。

日常交谈是练习的最好机会。日常交谈的场合也是你不断地作小型演讲的场合。最佳的现代演说方式不过是提升了规格的交谈活动。我指的并不是音调的提升，而是指建立在更高思想层次上比我们日常交谈的内容更精练的发言。

日常交谈也是帮你形成自己演讲风格的绝好机会。实际上,在交谈中形成的习惯会在演说中有意无意地表现出来，因为你平时讲话时多半也会面对一些听众。

所以，你应该看到在日常谈话中谨慎认真的重要性。要仔细地选择用词、注意发音与表达、嘴的张合要到位，这样你所说的词语便可以完全从嘴里出来，从而避免有些词的声音从鼻腔发出的现象。即使从谈话本身讲，也应该提倡谈话的素养,因为每个人即使不在公众场合讲话,也要与人私下交谈。

演讲自我训练的最好办法之一是大声朗诵一部收录精彩演讲稿的书,每天朗读几分钟。非常适合这种练习方法的汇编书籍有很多，关键是要按

pronunciation, expression, and gesture. These so-called mechanics should be developed until they become an unconscious part of the speaker's style.

Your best opportunity for practice is in your everyday conversation. There you are constantly making speeches on a small scale. Public speaking of the best modern type is simply elevated conversation. I do not mean elevated in pitch, but in the sense of being launched upon a higher level of thought and with greater intensity than is usually called for by ordinary conversation.

In conversation you have your best opportunity for developing your public speaking style. Indeed, you are there, despite yourself, forming habits which will disclose themselves in your public speaking. As you speak in your daily conversation you will largely speak when you stand before an audience.

You will therefore see the importance of care in your daily speech. There should be a fastidious choice of words, care in pronunciation and articulation, and the mouth well opened so that the words may come out wholly through the mouth and not partly through the nose. Culture of conversation is to be recommended for its own sake, since everyone must speak in private if not in public.

One of the best plans for self-culture in speaking is to read aloud for a few minutes every day from a book of well-selected speeches. There are numerous compilations of the kind admirably suited to this purpose. The important thing here is

演讲的方式去读，而不是用学校里通常传授的阅读方法。用这种方法练习时，最好想象自己正站在听众面前发表自己的演讲。演讲学习者要明智地避开矫揉造作的风格或其他怪癖。

另外一个好办法是在散步的时候在心里做简短的演讲。如果可能的话，最好找一条乡间小路、公园，或其他不会被路人分散注意力的地方。著名的英国演说家达弗林勋爵习惯在骑马时准备他绝大部分的演讲。养成做内心演讲的习惯对实际的口头演讲很有帮助，因为它能使人的思维充满活力及适应力，这是其他方法无法做到的。

画家、音乐家、雕刻家、建筑师及其他的工艺匠人为了学习和鼓舞自己都会找出仿效的榜样。演说者也应照此为之。历史表明世界上伟大的演说家也都是这么做的。把历史上最优秀的短篇演讲——林肯的葛底斯堡演讲当成典范是最好不过的了。

一个在英语文体方面的权威人士带着挑剔的目光研究了这篇演说并承认他难以建议做任何的修改，因为任何修改都无法再为它增加更强的影响力、使其更完善。

让我们回顾一下这篇演讲词的写作背景。1863

to read in speaking style, not in what is termed reading style as usually taught in schools. When you practise in this way it would be well to imagine an audience before you and to render the speech as if emanating from your own mind. The student of public speaking will wisely guard himself against acquiring an artificial style or other mannerism.

Another good plan is to make short mental speeches while walking. When possible it is well to choose a country road for this purpose, or a park, or some other place where one's mind is not likely to be often diverted by passers-by. Lord Dufferin, the eminent British orator, was accustomed to prepare most of his speeches while riding on horseback. The habit of forming mental speeches is a great aid to actual speech-making, as it tends to give the mind a power and an adaptability which it would not otherwise have.

The painter, the musician, the sculptor, the architect, and other craftsmen search out models for study and inspiration. The public speaker should do likewise, and history shows that the great orators of the world have followed this practise. You can not do better than take as your model the greatest short speech in all history, the Gettysburg Address.

An authority on English style has critically examined this speech and acknowledges that he cannot suggest a single change in it which would add to its power and perfection.

You recall the circumstances under which it was written. On the morning of November 18,

年 11 月 8 日的清晨，亚伯拉罕·林肯从华盛顿出发赶往葛底斯堡，去参加第二天举行的国家公墓祭奠活动。他将演讲词写在一张包装纸上，字斟句酌地仔细修改写、校正直至完成。

第二天，当这篇演讲发表之后，技巧精湛而老练的演说家爱德华·埃弗雷特说，如果他花两小时的演讲能达到林肯只花了两分钟的演讲效果的话，他便知足了。

认真地研究林肯这篇演讲词并探究它之所以具有影响力的最深处的奥秘会让你受益匪浅。这篇演说词最根本的特点当属难能可贵的简要朴实——观点简明、语言简洁、目的简单 ，而在通篇演讲中处处闪耀着的则是伟大的解放者林肯本人的简朴。

简要朴实是成功的演讲的显著特征之一，也是一切真正艺术的典型特点。它很微妙，难以解释清楚。但费内隆却帮我们给出了定义：简朴即是心灵的正直，是毫不考虑自己的品质。”它是无私的同义词。

在今天这个充斥着自我宣传和自我吹捧的社会里，能遇到一个真正简朴的人实在让人如沐春风。我们被他率真的态度、平和的说理、和蔼的语调、毫无偏见的观点和冷静的头脑所折服。我们为

1863, Abraham Lincoln was travelling from Washington to take part next day in the consecration of the national cemetery at Gettysburg. He wrote his speech on a scrap of wrapping–paper, carefully fitting word to word, changing and correcting it in minutest detail as best he could until it was finished.

The next day after the speech had been delivered, Edward Everett, the trained and polished orator, said that he would have been content to have made in his oration of two hours the impression which Lincoln had made in that many minutes.

It will repay you to study this speech closely and to wrest from it its innermost secrets of power and effectiveness. The greatest underlying quality of this speech is its rare simplicity—simplicity of thought, simplicity of language, simplicity of purpose, and shining through it all, the simplicity of the great emancipator himself.

This simplicity is one of the great distinguishing qualities of effective public speaking. It is characteristic of all true art. It is subtle and difficult to define, but Fénelon gives a definition that will aid us when he says, "Simplicity is an uprightness of soul that has no reference to self." It is another word for unselfishness.

In these days of self–exploitation and self–aggrandizement, how refreshing it is to meet a man of true simplicity. We are won by his unaffected manner, his gentleness of argument, his ingratiating tones of voice, his freedom from prejudice and

他的简朴的魅力所倾倒。

这种杰出的品质明显地表现在那些头脑清醒的人们身上。他们对生活有深刻的体验;他们懂得掌握分寸并且能够明察事理;他们能够按照事物的真正价值评价事物;他们镇定自若、有自制力、充满自信。他们有自知之明,并逐渐以朴实而闻名于世。

朴实不可与软弱或无知相混淆。朴实是一种必须长期地接受教育才能够获得的品质。它并不意味着迂腐平庸或者缺乏情趣,而是一种坚强刚毅的品质。倘若一个演讲家不具备这种朴实的品质,其他一切都无法弥补它的缺位。

朗费罗称它为至高的杰出品质,因为只有它能最有效地给人的心灵带来平静,能让生活充实而有意义。每个人都应力图认真地培养这种品质,因为它是高尚人格所必需的要素。

这篇演讲能够打动听众的的另外一个显著的特征是真诚。真诚主要来自朴实,是正直心灵的产物。尽管人们说不清这种特征的出处,却能很快辨认出来。我们发现在商界或是其他专业领域的杰出人物身上这一特征极为显著。如果一个人不真

passion. Such a man wins us almost wholly by the power of his simplicity.

This supreme quality is noticeable in men who are said to have come to themselves. They have tasted and tested life, they have learned proportion and perspective, they have appraised things at their real value, and now they carry themselves in poise and power and confidence. They have found themselves in a high and true sense, and they have come to be known as men of simplicity.

Simplicity is not to be confounded with weakness or ignorance. It comes through long education. It does not mean the trite, or the commonplace, or the obvious. It is a strong and sturdy quality, is this simplicity of which I am speaking, and nothing else will atone for lack of it in the public speaker.

Longfellow calls it the supreme excellence, since it is the quality which above all others brings serenity to the soul and makes life really worth living. Every man should earnestly seek to cultivate this great quality as essential to noble character.

This speech is conspicuous for another indispensable quality for effective public speaking,—the quality of sincerity. It grows largely out of simplicity and is the product of integrity of mind and heart. Men recognize it quickly, though they cannot easily tell whence it comes. We find it highly developed in great leaders in business and professional life. There has never been a really great public speaker who was not preeminently a

诚,那么他不可能成为真正伟大的演讲家。

比彻说:“不能让奸诈的小人成为演说家。”而事实上,这样的人也当不成演说家,因为人们很快便会发现他的真面目。世人对某个人的最终评价不会太离谱。

在华盛顿,一个很有前途的政治家正在对许多品位高雅的听众发表演说。歌剧院里座无虚席,显然他的演讲很受欢迎。但就在其演讲达到高潮时,在全场一千多双眼睛的注视下,他突然朝坐在附近包厢里的朋友使了个眼色。在那一瞬间,他未来的政治前途就像是遭遇了闪电袭击的花瓶一般被击得粉碎。就是那一瞬间的不诚恳让在场的目光敏锐的听众给他打了分,也决定了他的厄运。

葛底斯堡演讲的另一个特点是直截了当。演说者有着明确的目的,他清楚自己想讲什么,然后便一句不多也一句不少地讲了出来。

整个演讲紧扣主题绝无横枝斜蔓,没有弥补思想贫乏的衬饰之词,没有多余的冠冕堂皇的大话,也没有空洞的华丽辞藻或漂亮的笼统原则。

有多少发言者的发言是无的放矢!又有多少发言者已经在路上了,却不知身向何方!

如果这种直截了当的特点用在商务会谈、委员会会议、电话交谈或演讲中,全国每年将节省数

sincere man.

Beecher said, "Let no man who is a sneak try to be an orator." Such a man can not be. He will shortly be found out. The world's ultimate estimate of a man is not far wrong.

A politician of much promise was addressing a distinguished audience in Washington. The Opera House was crowded to the doors to hear him and apparently he was making a good impression upon all his hearers. But suddenly, at the very climax of his speech, while upwards of two thousand eyes were rivetted upon him, he was seen to wink at a personal friend of his sitting in a nearby box, and at that instant his future political prospects were shattered as a vase struck by lightning. In that single instant of insincerity he was appraised by that discriminating audience and his doom was sealed.

Still another great quality in the Gettysburg speech is its directness. The speaker had a clearly-defined purpose in view. He knew what he wanted to say, and he proceeded to say it—no more, and no less.

There was no straying away into by-paths, no padding of words to make up for shortage of ideas, no superfluous and big-sounding phrases, no empty rhetoric or glittering generalities.

How many speakers there are who aim at nothing and hit it. How many speakers there are who are on their way but do not know whither.

If this directness of quality were applied to talking in business, in committee meetings, in telephone conversations, in public speaking, it

百万句话、大量的时间和能量。

你会注意到这篇演讲词难得的简洁的特点。该演讲词为我们提供了一个例证，它证明如果一个人确切地知道他想讲什么，那么他只需用265个单词、短短的两分钟时间，就能把话清楚地讲完。

不应忘记的是，虽然林肯的这篇演讲词看起来似乎是信手轻松写成的，但是这却要归功于他对词汇及英语风格长年累月的刻苦钻研。

他在词汇上有很高的造诣，他痴迷词汇、经常查找适当的词、研究词的用法，终于使自己成为了词汇的大师。

经常认真地研习词汇、每天都有意识地把一些词添加到自己的词汇库中，这是每个人都应养成的有用的习惯。坚持一年之后，有这种习惯的人将会掌握丰富的词汇，想用时便可信手拈来。

结尾是一篇演讲词的关键部分，也是许多演讲者容易栽跟头的地方。无数的演讲都因结尾而功亏一篑。

最重要的一点是要事先决定好演讲的结尾部分总结出什么观点或启示，不要因临时的影响而改变主意。

一些发言者本来可以在最后作出有力的总结，但是又舍不得省去原先准备讲的任何东西，因

would save annually in this country millions of words and incalculable time and energy.

You will note that this speech has the rare quality of conciseness. We have an illustration here of how much a man can say in about 265 words and in the short space of two minutes, if he knows precisely what he wants to say.

It is well to bear in mind that although this speech was scribbled off with seeming ease, Lincoln owed his ability to do it to a long and painstaking study of words and English style.

He was a profound student of the dictionary. He steeped himself in words. He scrutinized words, he studied words, he made himself a master of words.

This is a valuable habit for every man to form,—to study words regularly and earnestly, and to add consciously to his working vocabulary a few words daily—so in the course of a year such a man will acquire a large and varied stock of words which will do his instant bidding.

The conclusion is a vital part of a speech. It is a place of peril to many a public speaker. Countless speeches have been ruined by a bad conclusion.

The most important thing here is that having decided beforehand upon the particular ideas or message with which you intend to conclude your speech, not to let any influence lead you away from this preconceived purpose.

Some speakers are about to conclude effectively but are unwilling to omit anything

此仍竭力回忆着所准备的点点滴滴。这样的演讲最终会使结尾显得松散凌乱。

不必把结束语的每句话都背下来，但是所要表达的观点应在大脑中有个明确的框架并清楚地储存在记忆中。应记住的不是词句，而是观点。

只要晓得你能够随意地运用这些明确的观点，而且能够圆满地结束自己的讲话，那么你必然就有了足够的自信，而这种自信对你会有巨大的帮助。

千万不要忘记结束发言的以下这条黄金规则：只要把演讲的重要的话都说完，就不要再多谈细枝末节或再叙述一个故事，或者说“还有一句话”，而是说完之后，马上住口，立即坐下。

which they have planned to give in their speech, and so continue in an endeavor to recall every item. At last such a speech has a loose and straggling ending.

The words of the conclusion need not be memorized, but the ideas should be definitely outlined in the mind and fixed in the memory, not as words, but as ideas.

The knowledge that you can turn at will to these definite ideas, and so bring your speech to a close, will confer upon you a degree of self-confidence which will be of immense service to you.

You should ever bear in mind this golden rule for the conclusion of your speech: When you have finished what you have of importance to say, do not be tempted to wander off into by-paths, or to tell an additional story, or to say "and one word more," but having finished your speech, stop on the instant and sit down.

10.

给谈话者的一些实用性建议

要竭力使自己的观点富有魅力，这样的观点有以下特点：明确、清晰、深刻、符合逻辑、发人深省、说服力强、精当明了、形象生动、新颖、耐人寻味、直言不讳、易懂、催人奋进、有启发作用、概括性强、切合实际。切忌晦涩、深奥、难懂、幼稚、无关紧要、浅显、无说服力、空泛、荒谬、模棱两可、夸大其词、意义不明、不切实际。

所选用的词应该：词义明确、朴实、自然、有切实的意义、有说服力、生动、恰当、悦耳，还要丰富多样。切忌选用那些生僻、粗俗、陈旧、怪诞、华而不实、专业性强、太长、口语色彩太浓、平淡无味的词语。

英语的应用风格要讲求：质朴、平易、准确、明晰、简洁、中肯、有力、形象、生动、修辞多样、优美、得体、流利、抑扬顿挫、言之有物、高尚、灵活、顺畅、庄重、精练、机敏、贴切、语调悦耳、雅致、品

10.

Practical Hints for Speakers

Cultivate as the most desirable thoughts those which are definite, clear, deep, logical, profound, strong, precise, impressive, original, significant, explicit, luminous, positive, suggestive, comprehensive, and practical. Resolutely avoid all thoughts which are uncertain, recondite, obscure, immature, unimportant, shallow, weak, visionary, absurd, vague, extravagant, indefinite, or impractical.

In your choice and use of words give preference to those which are definite, simple, real, significant, forcible, expressive, adequate, musical, varied, and copious. Avoid those which are foreign, slangy, obsolete, unusual, extravagant, technical, long, colloquial, or commonplace.

The most desirable qualities in the use of English are the simple, plain, exact, lucid, concise, trenchant, vigorous, impressive, lively, figurative, polished, graceful, fluent, rhythmical, copious, elevated, flexible, smooth, dignified, terse, epigrammatic, felicitous, euphonious, elegant, and

位高。而应摒弃的是：漫无边际、冗长、啰嗦、夸张、繁琐、模棱两可、无说服力、单调、松散、随便、枯燥、浮华、迂腐、傲慢、玩弄辞藻、大言不惭、矫揉造作、拘于形式、过分修饰、结结巴巴、沉闷无趣、不合语法、含糊其辞、不知所云。

说话时嗓音要清纯、浑厚、圆润、柔韧、洪亮、悦耳、清晰、感人、和谐、沉稳、有力、清脆、婉转、饱满、高亢、自然、柔美、有磁性、表达力强、有感染力和激情。应尽量不要使你的声音刺耳、带喘气声、尖厉、粗哑、呆板、带喉音、粗嘎、微弱无力、尖细、带鼻音、不悦耳、不和谐、低沉、忽高忽低、不自然、听不清、沉闷、声嘶力竭、阴沉忧郁、颤抖。

吐字要清楚无误。避免随随便便、无精打采、咕咕哝哝、有气无力或语调夸张。

发音要清楚准确。切忌含糊不清、咬舌、不干脆、结结巴巴、卖弄炫耀、遗漏音节、吃掉词的最后一个辅音。

发表演说时，讲话的方式和风格要质朴、真诚、自然、多样、有魅力、诚恳、有打动人心的力量、能引发兴趣、令人振奋、活力四射、富有同情心、

lofty. Undesirable qualities are the diffuse, verbose, redundant, inflated, prolix, ambiguous, feeble, monotonous, loose, slip-shod, dry, flowery, pedantic, pompous, rhetorical, grandiloquent, artificial, formal, ornate, halting, ponderous, ungrammatical, vague, and obscure.

The qualities you should develop in your speaking voice are the pure, deep, round, flexible, resonant, musical, clear, sympathetic, smooth, sonorous, powerful, silvery, melodious, full, strong, natural, mellow, magnetic, expressive, carrying, and responsive. Endeavor to keep your voice free from such undesirable qualities as the harsh, breathy, sharp, rough, rigid, throaty, guttural, thin, shrill, nasal, unmusical, discordant, muffled, explosive, strained, inaudible, hollow, strident, sepulchral, and tremulous.

Your articulation should be clear, distinct, and correct. Avoid carelessness, lifelessness, mumbling, weakness, and exaggeration.

Your pronunciation should be clear-cut and accurate. Avoid mouthing, lisping, hesitation, stammering, pedantry, omission of syllables, and suppression of final consonants.

Your delivery in public speaking should be simple, sincere, natural, varied, magnetic, earnest, forceful, attractive, energetic, animated, sympathetic,

有权威性、不失尊严、直率、感人、生动、令人信服、说服力强、诚恳、热情、能鼓舞人心。切忌胆小羞怯、熟不拘礼、言辞过激、态度冷漠、麻木不仁、虚情假意、矫揉造作、沉闷乏味、节奏单调、支支吾吾、缺乏生气、无说服力、缺乏感情、声音平淡、自以为是、拘谨刻板、出尔反尔、油嘴滑舌、卖弄炫耀、拖腔拿调、无精打采。

姿势要优美、得体、大方、端正、自然。切忌做无意义的动作,或者姿势僵硬、粗俗、拘束、做作、生硬。

表情要丰富、适度、甜美、热情。切忌愁眉苦脸,或者表情呆板、单调。

站姿要有男子气概、挺直、大方、威严、令人肃然起敬。切忌萎靡不振、两脚移来移去、身体僵硬、一动不动、样子笨拙。

authoritative, dignified, direct, impressive, vivid, convincing, persuasive, zealous, enthusiastic, and inspiring. Avoid that which is timid, familiar, violent, cold, indifferent, unreal, artificial, dull, sing –song, hesitating, feeble, unconvincing, apathetic, monotonous, pompous, formal, arbitrary, flippant, ostentatious, drawling, or languid.

Your gesture should be graceful, appropriate, free, forceful, and natural. Avoid all gesture which is unmeaning, angular, abrupt, constrained, stilted, or amateurish.

Your facial expression should be varied, appropriate, pleasing, and impassioned. Avoid the unpleasant, immobile, and unvaried.

Let your standing position be manly, erect, easy, forceful, and impressive. Avoid that which is weak, shifting, stiff, inactive, and ungainly.

11.

谈话中的“表演性”因素

有人十分明确地反对把带有“表演性”的一些东西掺进讲经布道里。因为演员的技艺与牧师的活儿完全不是一回事儿。演员充其量不过是再现、模仿、扮演或者说表演。演员是假戏真做，而牧师则是真戏真做。

然而，恐怕就是这种偏见致使许多牧师缩手缩脚，布道时几乎没有什么热情和动作。他们尽量避免自己的布道带有表演和煽情的色彩，因此便克制自己，绕开了许多很自然、很有效的表达方式。布道的作用不仅仅是传教，还要说服听众；而说服听众所需要的不只是简单地动嘴说话、理智地叙述事实或朗读书面的教义。在牧师希望成功地说服并鼓舞听众之前，他还需要面部、眼睛、手臂乃至全身的积极配合，来表明他本人是深深地为教义的内容所打动的。

11.

The Dramatic Element in Speaking

There is a well–defined prejudice against the importation of anything "theatrical" into the pulpit. The art of the actor is fundamentally different from the work of the preacher. At best the actor but represents, imitates, pretends, acts. The actor seems; the preacher is.

It is to be feared, however, that this prejudice has narrowed many preachers down to a pulpit style almost devoid of warmth and action. In their endeavor to avoid the dramatic and sensational, they have refined and subdued many of their most natural and effective means of expression. The function of preaching is not only to impart, but to persuade; and persuasion demands something more than an easy conversational style, an intellectual statement of facts, or the reading of a written message. The speaker must show in face, in eye, in arm, in the whole animated man, that he, himself, is moved, before he can hope successfully to persuade and inspire others.

日常谈话中有限的动作并不能满足牧师的全部要求。这些动作只能满足布道的基本要求，但是到了需要激情的高潮阶段，当牧师的灵魂似乎要跳出躯体竭力进入听众的内心时，就必须有生机勃勃的活力和动作——“表演性”的动作来配合。

乔治·威廉·柯蒂斯给予温德尔·菲利普斯的高度称赞可谓绝无先例。乔治·威廉·柯蒂斯写道：“他完全沉浸在自己的神圣信仰之中，他

‘热血沸腾，表情丰富，

激动之情楚楚昭昭，

仿佛连他的身体都在思考’。”

稳重即力量；矜持、克制也是牧师神圣工作的组成部分，但是如果矜持克制得过了头，它们就可能变质为软弱无力、徒劳无用的东西。规范的英语、华丽的修辞以及深刻的思想都不能完全弥补讲话时适当的动作的缺失。

下述的例子足以清楚地说明动作本身的力量：手指触唇表示请安静，指向门表示命令某人出去。牧师可能常常发现有一种做法很有好处，即站在镜子前仅用手势动作来讲经说道，以检验一下自己布道的效力。

身体的动作跟讲话者所运用的其他手段一样

The modified movements of ordinary conversation do not fulfil all the requirements of the preacher. These are necessary and adequate for the groundwork of the sermon, but for the supreme heights of passionate appeal, when the soul of the preacher would, as it were, leap from its body in the endeavor to reach men, there must be intensified life and action—dramatic action.

It is difficult to conceive of a greater tribute to a public advocate than that paid to Wendell Phillips by George William Curtis:" The divine energy of his conviction utterly possest him, and his

'Pure and eloquent blood
Spoke in his cheek, and so distinctly wrought,
That one might almost say his body thought.'"

Poise is power, and reserve and repression are parts of the dignified office of the preacher, but carried too far may degenerate into weak and unproductive effort. Perfection of English style, rhetorical floridness, and profundity of thought will never wholly make up for lack of appropriate action in the work of persuading men.

The power of action alone is vividly illustrated in the touch of the finger to the lips to invoke silence, or the pointing to the door to command one to leave the room. The preacher might often find it profitable to stand before a mirror and deliver his sermon exclusively in pantomime to test its power and efficacy.

The body must be disciplined and cultivated as assiduously as the other instruments of the

也必需勤练。姿态和动作的说服力并不亚于声音与情绪。当所有的其他方法都不管用时，牧师可以挺直身体，将头意味深长地摇一摇或者将警告的目光射向听众，也许就会使他们把注意力转到听布道上来。

60年前，威廉·拉塞尔牧师就强调过表情的重要性。提到传教士，他说："他的外在形象从姿势到动作如同他的声音都应富于变化：他会用身体的姿态去引导听众的情绪；当崇拜之辞说出口时，他那慢慢向上举起的手即表示他的内心充满了郑重的敬畏；作为基督的使者，向同胞们传达上帝的旨意时，其宽厚诚挚之情及劝说之意将通过他那祈求的手势和神态表现出来；他还应知道如何对该受谴责的有罪之人表现出权威的严厉态度；在适当的时机，他会通过激动的神态、令人鼓舞的姿势向听众表明他背负着振奋人类灵魂的神圣使命；他用柔和低沉的话语将自己的同情送入哀悼者的内心；他噙泪的双眸和温柔的动作表现出他对受苦受难民众的恻隐之心；总之，他整个的内心世界都清楚地表现在他的表情、姿态和富有说服力的手势之中；他总的传教风格给人的感觉是心与心

speaker. There is eloquence of attitude and action no less than eloquence of voice and feeling. A preacher drawing himself up to his full height, with a significant gesture of the head, or with flashing eye pointing the finger of warning at his hearers, may rouse them from indifference when all other means fail.

Sixty years ago the Reverend William Russell emphasized the importance of visible expression. He said of the preacher:"His outward manner, in attitude and action, will be as various as his voice: he will evince the inspiration of appropriate feeling in the very posture of his frame; in uttering the language of adoration, the slow-moving, uplifted hand will bespeak the awe and solemnity which pervade his soul; in addressing his fellow men in the spirit of an ambassador of Christ, the gentle yet earnest spirit of persuasive action will be evinced in the pleading hand and aspect; he will know, also, how to pass to the stern and authoritative mien of the reproved of sin; he will, on due occasions, indicate, in his kindling look, the rousing gesture, the mood of him who is empowered and commanded to summon forth all the energies of the human soul; his subdued and chastened address will carry the sympathy of his spirit into the bosom of the mourner; his moistening eye and his gentle action will manifest his tenderness for the suffering: his whole soul will, in a word, become legible in his features, in his attitude, in the expressive eloquence of his hand; his whole style will be felt to be that of heart communing with

的交流。”

“表演性”的动作使口头言辞变得形象生动。对想象力迟缓的听众来说，它会让所说的事物变得鲜活清晰，与没有动作配合相比，它为讲话者传达的信息注入了新的意义和活力。同时也展现了讲话者对自己的听众感情上的契合与支持。他的思想和情感与声音、表情、手势、身体的姿态和动作结合起来，达到充分、完整表达的效果，从而使听众满意并且给他们留下深刻印象。

亨利·沃德·比彻就是一个典型的例子，他的布道具有“表演”风格。读大学期间，在嗓音修养、姿势和动作上他接受了三年的训练。他每天都在树林中练习每个元音的发音，声音由最低到最高。这种练习不仅给了他一副灵敏、柔韧的好嗓子，而且使他能自如地运用肢体动作，这让他成了美国最有布道实力的传教士中的一员。他的确是一位高水平的布道演说家。

聪明的牧师要避免显得怪模怪样和活泼过度。不停地打手势和做动作、用手和头部动作进行过分的强调以及一切显得妄自尊大的姿势和动作都应该避免。各种各样的表达手段都应准备好以便随时可用。不过，这些手段的运用要得体、有品位，那才是一个稳健的人的特征。过多的动作和时间太长的激情“表演”会失去效力。除非把作用力和反作用力定律运用于传经布道中，否则听布道

heart."

Dramatic action gives picturesqueness to the spoken word. It makes things vivid to slow imaginations, and by contrast invests the speaker's message with new meaning and vitality. It discloses, too, the speaker's sympathy and identification with his subject. His thought and feeling, communicating themselves to voice and face, to hand and arm, to posture and walk, satisfy and impress the hearer by a sense of adequacy and completeness.

Henry Ward Beecher, a conspicuous example of the dramatic style in preaching, was drilled for three years, while at college, in voice-culture, gesture, and action. His daily practise in the woods, during which he exploded all the vowels from the bottom to the top of his voice, gave him not only a wonderfully responsive and flexible instrument, but a freedom of bodily movement that made him one of the most vigorous and virile of American preachers. He was in the highest sense a persuasive pulpit orator.

A sensible preacher will avoid the grotesque and the extremes of mere animal vivacity. Incessant gesture and action, undue emphasizing with hand and head, and all suggestion of self-sufficiency in attitude or manner should be guarded against. All the various instruments of expression should be made ready and responsive for immediate use, but are to be employed with that taste and tact that characterize the well-balanced man. Too much action and long-continued emotional effort lose force, and unless the law of action and reaction is

的会众的注意力将很快他顾，而预想的效果也会彻底毁灭。

脸作为情感的镜子是不可或缺的表情部位。嘴唇能显示坚定、悲伤、怜悯、慈爱或讲话人的其他情感。眼睛是显示心灵的最直接的媒介，气愤时它怒火炎炎、高兴时它熠熠生辉、悲伤时则黯淡无光。而眉毛呢，惊讶时它会高挑，决心下定和困惑时则会下垂。

布道时突然压低声音的效果不可忽视。如果谨慎使用这种方法，或许牧师的话会给听众留下更深刻、更严肃的印象，或者会让会众中那些心不在焉的人重新集中精力。

要获得以情动人的能力、掌握“表演性”的动作，牧师应该研究一下优秀的剧作家。他应该用恰如其分的声音再配上适当的动作朗读他们的作品。他还应该研究儿童、成人、以及世间常情。他或许还应该去看一看最出色的演员的表演，当然不是为着完全模仿他们，而是为着让他们激发自己的审美情趣和想象力。

applied to the preaching of the sermon the attention of the congregation may snap and the desired effect be utterly destroyed.

The face as the mirror of the emotions is an important part of expression. The lips will betray determination, grief, sympathy, affection, or other feeling on the part of the speaker. The eyes, the most direct medium of psychic power, will flash in indignation, glisten in joy, or grow dim in sorrow. The brow will be elevated in surprise, or lowered in determination and perplexity.

The effectiveness of the whisper in preaching should not be overlooked. If discreetly used it may serve to impress the hearer with the profundity and seriousness of the preacher's message, or to arrest and bring back to the point of contact the wandering minds of a congregation.

To acquire emotional power and dramatic action the preacher should study the great dramatists. He should read them aloud with appropriate voice and movement. He should study children, and men, and nature. He should, perhaps, see the best actors, not to copy them, but in order that they may stimulate his taste and imagination.

12.

日常谈话与演讲

公开演说的理想风格其实就是稍加改变的有效的日常谈话式的风格。我们生活的这个时代需要的是口语风格的演说，而不是传统的演说风格的演讲。在日常谈话中，有话可说的人通常都能侃侃而谈。如果他在介绍事实，他会说得头头是道；如果他表达出恳切之情，听众一定会情不自禁地被他感染；如果他是一个有学识的人，他的言辞无疑会显得文质彬彬。

在有教养的孩子们的日常谈话中，我们可以发现他们那率真的言辞既十分有趣又十分有效。那抑扬顿挫的优美语调、着重语气的自然而准确的使用以及真挚深沉的情感完全可以成为比他们年长的演说者的榜样。

对我们自己和他人的日常谈话的这种研究给我们提供了日常练习的机会，从而使我们的讲话变得更准确、更流畅。我们所研究的是在日常谈话

12.

Conversation and Public Speaking

The ideal style of public speaking is, with very little modification, the ideal of good conversation. The practical age in which we live demands a colloquial rather than an oratorical style of public speaking. A man who has something to say in conversation usually has little difficulty in saying it. If he presents the facts he will speak convincingly; if he is deeply in earnest he will speak persuasively; and if he be an educated man his speech will have the unmistakable marks of culture and refinement.

In the conversation of well-bred children we find the most interesting and helpful illustrations of unaffected speech. The exquisite modulation of the voice, the unstudied correctness of emphasis, and the sincerity and depth of feeling might well serve as a model for older speakers.

This study of conversation, both our own and that of others, offers daily opportunity for improvement in accuracy and fluency of speech, of

中如何用贴切的词表达思想，以及如何养成好的讲话习惯，这样的习惯会不知不觉地表现在面对更多听众的演讲中。日常谈话中谨慎的习惯可以使演讲者避免在演讲时语气夸张做作，也可以使他即使在需要着重处理的内容上仍然神态自若。

以下是一些很容易就可记住的有关日常谈话的建议：

1.吐字要清楚准确，要像铸币厂“新出的钢镚儿”似的那么清脆响亮，但是切忌故弄玄虚。

2. 任何时候都不讲漫不经心的话或不妥当的话。

3.日常谈话中口形要到位。吐字不清主要是由于嘴欲张不张的缘故。

4. 严格要求自己并且观察他人的日常谈话方式，找出不妥之处并改进自己的讲话方式。

5.思想的表达要由多种语气来配合。声音的抑扬顿挫需要声音的高低、发音的力度、谈问题的角度、语气中的情感都有适当的变化。

6.切忌谈话时嗓门过大。

7.只要把辅音发好，元音则不成问题。

8.在日常谈话中要培养抑扬顿挫的语调。

9.声音要浑厚有力才好。

10.记住在日常谈话这件事上进行有意识的练

fitting words to the mouth as well as to the thought, and of forming habits that will unconsciously disclose themselves in the larger work of public speaking. Care in conversation will guard the public speaker from inflated and unnatural tones, and restrain him from transgressing the laws of nature even in those parts of his speech demanding lofty and intensified treatment.

Some easily remembered suggestions regarding conversation are these:

1.Pronounce your words distinctly and accurately, like "newly made coins" from the mint, but without pedantry.

2.Upon no occasion allow yourself to indulge in careless or incorrect speech.

3.Open the mouth well in conversation. Much indistinct speech is due to speaking through half–closed teeth.

4.Closely observe your conversation and that of others, to detect faults and to improve your speaking–style.

5.Vary your voice to suit the variety of your thought. A well –modulated voice demands appropriate changes of pitch, force, perspective, and feeling.

6.Avoid loud talking.

7.Take care of the consonants and the vowels will take care of themselves.

8.Cultivate the music of the conversational tones.

9.Favor the low pitches of your voice.

10.Remember that the purpose of conscious

习和观察，为的是最终无意识地实际运用。

将得体的日常谈话的风格作为有效的演讲风格是很有用的一种演讲方式，但是却很少有人能认识到它的价值。比彻说：“白白浪费了多少声音啊！”他指的就是人们通常忽略了这种能提高自己演讲能力的宝贵机会。不过多啰嗦几句也不算过分的是，假如牧师能够把在日常谈话中听到的母亲们说话的甜美、温柔，父亲们说话的坚定、慈爱，孩子们说话的自然、悦耳都融于自己的声音里并且用于布道，那么他的布道无疑会在听众心中产生神奇而持久的作用。牧师布道时所需的是恋人求爱的语调，而不是发表宣言或训斥谴责的腔调。

研究日常谈话不仅可以帮助演讲者演说时自如地运用嗓音和表情，而且还可以帮助他把话说好。在日常谈话中，他会学会选用简单的而不是复杂的词、选用短句而不是结构复杂的长句、选择具体明了的例证而不是抽象模糊的例证。他会养成轻松、自如、朴实、直率的讲话风格，并且当他站起身来发表演讲时，他会使用人们熟悉的语调和易懂的言辞。

牧师在书房独处的时间可能太长了。果真如此的话，那么他很快就会认识到自己因缺乏与同

practise and observation in the matter of conversation is to lead ultimately to unconscious performance.

The value of correct conversation as a means to effective public speaking is realized by few men. Beecher said: "How much squandering there is of the voice!" meaning that this golden opportunity for improvement was generally disregarded. It is not too much to say, however, that if the sweet and gentle expression of the mother, the strong and affectionate tones of the father, and the spontaneous musical notes of the children, as heard in daily conversation, could be united in the voice of the minister and brought to the preaching of his sermon, there would be little doubt of its magical and enduring effect upon the hearts of men. The wooing tone of the lover is what the preacher needs in his pulpit style rather than the voice of declamation and denunciation.

The study of conversation serves to guide the public speaker not only in the free and natural use of his voice, enunciation, and expression, but also in his use of language. He will here learn to choose the simple word instead of the complex, the short sentence instead of the involved, the concrete illustration instead of the abstract. He will acquire ease, spontaneity, simplicity, and directness, and when he rises to speak to men he will employ tones and words best known and understood by them.

A preacher may spend too much time in study and solitude. If he does he will soon realize

胞们的社交活动而造成的明显损失。布道最需要的能力主要是在日常谈话中练就的能力。敏捷的思维能力、梳理事实和论点的能力、讲一个生动的故事或实例的能力、为了坚持原则有时需绕开话题或进行抨击的能力，以及日常谈话中常有的动脑筋的锻炼，所有这些都往往有助于形成风趣、活泼、有力的演讲风格。

我们不能低估演讲者沉思和默想的益处。它们是探索新颖深刻的见解、开发想象力和积累思考成果所必不可少的。不过，谈话则为沉思所积累下的知识提供了直接的输出途径，同时通过表达还可以对思考的成果进行检验，也就是通过嗓音和情感的帮助将其投射到生活和现实中去。日常谈话的锻炼是益智所必需的，犹如体育锻炼是健身所必不可少的一样。的确，满载的头脑需要通过表达来减轻负担，否则压力会变得不堪重负。

日常谈话的位置不应被日报和杂志夺走。假如像某些人所宣称的那样谈话的艺术正在很快地消亡，那么我们就应该尽自己的力量使其再生。也许往日谈话中的机智幽默、妙语巧辩、精彩的唇枪舌剑已不可复得，但我们每个人至少还可以拥有优雅的语调、风趣地表达观点的方式和母语的纯正发音。

a distinct loss through lack of social intercourse with his fellow men. The faculties most needed in pulpit preaching are those very powers that are so largely exercised in ordinary conversation. The ability to think quickly, to marshal facts and arguments, to introduce a vivid story or illustration, to parry and thrust as is sometimes needed to hold one's own ground, and the general mental activity aroused in conversation, all tend to produce an interesting, vivacious, and forceful style in public speaking.

We should not underestimate the value of meditation and silence to the public speaker. These are necessary for original and profound thinking, for the cultivation of the imagination, and for the accumulation of thought. But conversation offers an immediate outlet for this stored-up knowledge, testing it as a finished product in expression, and projecting it into life and reality by all the resources of voice and feeling. This exercise is as necessary to the mind as physical exercise is to the body. Indeed, a full mind demands this relief in expression, lest the strain become too great.

The daily newspaper and the magazines should not be allowed to usurp the place of conversation. If the art of talking is rapidly dying out, as some assert, we should do our share to revive it. We may not again have the wit and repartee, the brilliant intellectual combats of those other days, but we can at least each have a cultivated speaking-voice, an interesting manner of expressing our ideas in conversation, and a refined pronunciation of our mother tongue.

13.

讲给牧师的话

以发言的方式给别人讲解文学，主讲人应首先吸收文学的精髓。如果对一部优秀的诗歌选集或散文选集的作品涵义与要旨缺乏透彻的理解，就不会谈出什么有价值或令人满意的见解。透彻的理解是避免呆板空洞的高谈阔论的主要办法。对作品思想内在实质的理解与掌握程度基本上能决定你的话里含有多少对生活与现实的感悟以及含有多少感人的成分。

讲话人的声音和情绪之间的密切关系表明两者是相辅相成的。声音只能说出说话人头脑里已经意识到的东西，因此说话人用自己的话所表达出的意思也最准确地反映了他对其中问题的理解程度。正是这种主要来自直觉和情感的精神力量给谈话增添了不寻常的魅力，而且这也是比逻辑、修辞和学识更有效的东西，它能使讲话人更容易

13.

A Talk to Preachers

The aim of one who would interpret literature to others, by means of the speaking voice, should be first to assimilate its spirit. There can be no worthy or adequate rendering of a great poem or prose selection without a keen appreciation of its inner meaning and content. This is the principal safeguard against mechanical and meaningless declamation. The extent of this appreciation and grasp of the inherent spirit of thought will largely determine the degree of life, reality, and impressiveness imparted to the spoken word.

The intimate relationship between the voice and the spirit of the speaker suggests that one is necessary to the fullest development of the other. The voice can interpret only what has been awakened and realized within, hence nothing discloses a speaker's grasp of a subject so accurately and readily as his attempt to give it expression in his own language. It is this spiritual power, developed principally through the intuitions and emotions, that gives psychic force to speaking, and which more than logic, rhetoric, or learning itself

地影响听众的情感并说服他们。

牧师是至高无上的神圣真理的解说者，因此他布道时要感情充沛、声音悦耳。光是清楚、有力地说明道理还不够，他还必须满腔热忱、慷慨激昂地去宣讲才能打动听众。为了充分表达神圣真理的无穷内涵，他必须能够驾驭自己的声音，就像能自如地弹奏教堂的管风琴一样，既能奏出“充满爱的柔和琴声”，也能奏出“高亢的军号声”。

有人以为学习了说话的艺术在公开演讲时就势必会总想着它的规则；也有人说知道了语法、修辞或逻辑规则之后，教师、作家、思想家讲话就势必会矫揉造作；其实前者跟后者一样，都是毫无根据的。正如歌德所言“熟练的技巧是第一位的，艺术是第二位的”，这不仅适用于音乐家、艺术家、演员和文学家，也适用于演说家。

如果牧师每天挺胸鼓肚地站五分钟，同时用不同的力度和感情大声发英语中的长元音，过不了多久他就会发现自己的声音变得富有弹性、能引发共鸣并且铿然有力。要记住声音是在运用中培养出来的。如果牧师也能养成休息时只用鼻孔

enables the speaker to influence and persuade men.

The minister as an interpreter of the highest spiritual truth should bring to his work a thoroughly trained emotional nature and a cultivated speaking voice. It is not sufficient that he state the truth with clearness and force; he must proclaim it with such passionate enthusiasm as powerfully to move his hearers. To express adequately the infinite shades of spiritual truth, he must have the ability to play upon his voice as upon a great cathedral organ, from "the soft lute of love" to "the loud trumpet of war."

To assume that the study of the art of speaking will necessarily produce consciousness of its principles while in the act of speaking in public, is as unwarranted as to say that a knowledge of the rules of grammar, rhetoric, or logic lead to artificiality and self-consciousness in the teacher, writer, and thinker. There is a " mechanical expertness preceding all art," as Goethe says, and this applies to the orator no less than to the musician, the artist, the actor, and the litterateur.

Let the minister stand up for even five minutes each day, with chest and abdomen well expanded, and pronounce aloud the long vowel sounds of the English language, in various shades of force and feeling, and shortly he will observe his voice developing in flexibility, resonance, and power. For it should be remembered that the voice grows through use. Let the minister cultivate, too, the habit of breathing exclusively through his nose while in repose, fully and deeply from the

深呼吸的习惯，那么他会发现自己身心的健康将有明显改善。

讲话人要想在精神和情感修养上得到更大的提高,广泛多样的人生知识是必备的。情感的成熟需要深入了解人类的疾苦、需要参与重大社会问题的解决和处理。在诠释别人内心的秘密之前,讲话人最好先探索自己的内心世界并努力解读其中的秘密。亲身体验痛苦比读书更容易找到心灵之源。

然而我们必须注意培养感情要沿着理性的路线前行,以免误入歧途,陷入狂热的泥潭。刻意展示的激情或只追求一时效果的激情与源自内心强烈信念以及对他人关切的激情是有天壤之别的。虚伪、做作的感情一定不会让那些严肃的人们信服。

肯纳德博士说:“无缘无故地激动亢奋对人的心理常情既是一种不敬也是一种伤害。”当听众的注意力完全被吸引住时，每一位听众就像一架调好音的竖琴,每一根弦都代表一种情感,技巧娴熟的讲话人可以随心所欲地拨动其中的一根或几根。这使他肩负起严肃的重大责任。此时,他应该镇定地把握住自己神圣的目的，以便使自己的行为是健康的行为、使自己的生命与上帝的旨意相配、

abdomen, and he will find himself gaining in health and mental resourcefulness.

For the larger development of the spiritual and emotional powers of the speaker, a wide and varied knowledge of men and life is necessary. The feelings are trained through close contact with human suffering, and in the work of solving vital social problems. The speaker will do well to explore first his own heart and endeavor to read its secret meanings, preliminary to interpreting the hearts of other men. Personal suffering will do more to open the well-springs of the heart than the reading of many books.

Care must be had, however, that this cultivating of the feelings be conducted along rational lines, lest it run not to faith but to fanaticism. There is a wide difference between emotion designed for display or for momentary effect, and that which arises from strong inner conviction and sympathetic interest in others. Spurious, unnatural feeling will invariably fail to convince serious-minded men.

"Emotion wrought up with no ulterior object," says Dr. Kennard, "is both an abuse and an injury to the moral nature. When the attention is thoroughly awakened and steadily held, the hearer is like a well-tuned harp, each cord a distinct emotion, and the skilful speaker may evoke a response from one or more at his will. This lays him under a great and serious responsibility. Let him keep steadily at such a time to his divine purpose, to produce a healthful action, a life in

使自己的努力成为对人类做出的贡献。

每天从《圣经》、莎士比亚作品中摘录雄辩有力且热情洋溢的一段话高声朗读或朗读布什内尔、纽曼、比彻、麦克拉伦、布鲁克斯或是斯珀吉翁等人的一些经典传教片段，这样便可以充实讲话人的情感和精神力量。人类的全部情感都可以通过高声朗读经典文学作品得到极大的升华。如果讲话人首先用这种方式对自己进行了检验和训练，他就会发现他也能够让自己的言辞变得很精彩、很生动。此外，通过对词语的斟酌和对他人情感的吸收，当他试图说出自己的想法时，他表达的流利程度和嗓音的敏感程度都将得到极大的改善。

音乐是唤起讲话人的情感、让讲话人感觉到自己隐秘心声的一个强有力因素。牧师不光要多听优美的音乐，而且要训练自己的耳朵，使其能识别言语中的节奏和韵调。

要想充分提高心理素质，演讲人就得耐得住寂寞。要想有较多的收获就必须多听。思想和情感的成熟是需要时间的。这样，讲话人的内心就会捕捉到人类和大自然极为丰富的声音，随后他会把这些声音传达给他人。

harmony with God and a symphony of service."

The emotional and spiritual powers of the speaker will be developed by reading aloud each day a vigorous and passionate extract from the Bible, or Shakespeare, or from some great sermon by such men as Bushnell, Newman, Beecher, Maclaren, Brooks, or Spurgeon. The entire gamut of human feeling can be highly cultivated by thus reading aloud from the great masterpieces of literature. The speaker will know that he can make his own words glow and vibrate, after he has first tested and trained himself in some such manner as this. Furthermore, by thus fitting words to his mouth, and assimilating the feelings of others, he will immeasurably gain in facility and vocal responsiveness when he attempts to utter his own thoughts.

Music is a powerful element in awakening emotion in the speaker and bringing to consciousness the mysterious inner voices of the soul. The minister should not only hear good music as often as possible, but he should train his ear to recognize the rhythm and melody in speech.

For the fullest development of this spiritual power in the public speaker there should be frequent periods of stillness and silence. One must listen much in order to accumulate much. Thought and feeling require time in which to grow. In this way the myriad sounds that arise from humanity and from nature can be caught up in the soul of the speaker and subsequently voiced by him to others.

习惯针对自己或他人的观点沉思默想的人常常会发现更深层的新内涵，其情感也因此会变得更加细腻深沉。讲话人要孜孜不倦地寻找未用言语写出的事物的内涵；因此他应经常研究经典的绘画和雕塑，他还需密切观察那些有良好教养的儿童在谈话中自然流露出的情感；同时还有许多其他随时想到的方法，讲话人要通过这些方法每天增益自己说话时感情和精神上的力量。

布道的科学性很重要，不过布道的艺术性也很重要。时代需要影响力巨大的讲道坛。教会的会众乐于接受有坚定信念、以慈悲为怀、人格圣洁的牧师。牧师慈善的性情将从他的声音、表情和动作上表现出来，正是这种天性吸引并影响着人们，而苛刻、生硬、暴躁的态度则很容易使人们产生反感。

令人堪忧的是许多布道稿的撰写偏重于“书面的文采”，而对其作为演讲需感动人的重要性则考虑甚少。

牧师要做到对自己的观点坚信不疑，要以炽热的感情把它牢牢记在心中，这样他才能够再把它明确而理直气壮地传达给其他人。观点原本就模糊不清、自己心里就犹犹豫豫，讲出来时也同样会模糊、犹豫。在撰写布道稿时，要把稿子写得生

The habit of meditating much, of brooding over thought, whether it be our own or that of others, will tend to disclose new and deeper meanings, and consequently deeper shades and depths of feeling. The speaker will diligently search for unwritten meanings in words; he will study, whenever possible, masterpieces of painting and sculpture; he will closely observe the natural feeling of well-bred children, as shown in their conversation; and in many other ways that will suggest themselves, he will daily develop his emotional and spiritual powers of expression.

The science of preaching is important, but so, too, is the art of preaching. A powerful pulpit is one of the needs of the times. A congregation readily recognizes a preacher of strong convictions, broad sympathies, and consecrated personality. An affectionate nature in a minister, manifesting itself in voice, face, and manner, will attract and influence men, while a harsh, rigid, vehement manner will as easily repel them.

It is to be feared that many sermons are written with too much regard for "literary deportment on paper," and too little thought of their value as pulsating messages to men.

The preacher should train himself to take tight hold of his thought, to grip it with mental firmness and fervor, that he may afterward convey it to others with definiteness and vigor. Thoughts vaguely conceived and held tremblingly in the mind will manifest a like character when uttered. Into the writing of the sermon put vitality and

动、充满激情，那么布道时这样的特点也会自然地表现出来。要想讲得好，就必须先把讲稿写好。牧师可以模仿狄更斯创作小说人物时的习惯，在写布道稿的过程中，他可以不时地站起来冲着想象中的教会会众大声说出自己的想法以检验其力度和效果。

牧师一定要全面提高自己的涵养，这样才能把精神和情感的力量调动出来并控制在手中，以便需要时能够立即做出准确的反应。要刻苦地训练自己的声音，使其成为表达的得力工具和抒发思想情感的自然渠道。把表达的两种关键的东西（心里素质和嗓音）训练好并结合在一起，牧师就会发现讲经说道的真正秘诀。

intensity, and these qualities will find their natural place in delivery. Thrill of the pen should precede thrill of the voice. The habit of Dickens of acting out the characters he was depicting on paper could be copied to advantage by the preacher, and frequently during the writing of his sermon he might stand and utter his thoughts aloud to test their power and effectiveness upon an imaginary congregation.

There should be the most thorough cultivation of the inner sources of the preacher, whereby the spiritual and emotional forces are so aroused and brought under control as to respond promptly and accurately to all the speaker's requirements. There should be assiduous training of the speaking voice as the instrument of expression and the natural outlet for thought and feeling. In the combined cultivation of these two essentials of expression—spirit and voice—the minister will find the true secret of effective pulpit preaching.

14.

讲话人要保护好自己的嗓子

对演讲者而言，喉咙是演讲的关键部位，因此非常值得保养爱护。令人感到吃惊的是，虽然人们知道如果嗓子不响亮或者有病，就可能导致讲话人无法胜任重要的演讲任务，但人们还是不太注意喉咙保健。娇嫩、复杂的发音器官特别怕使用不当或保护不力。常见的缺陷有鼻音重、嗓音沙哑或刺耳，这些都是由于嗓子运用不当而造成的。

在训练中，演讲者首先要做的就是控制好自己的呼吸器官。也就是说，演讲者要通过认真的练习使自己习惯于用腹部用力由鼻孔呼吸，这样可以避免常会出现的喉咙负担过重的问题。这种呼吸方式并不难掌握，因为它只是要求吸气时肚子

14.

Care of the Speaker's Throat

The throat as a vital part of the public speaker's work in speaking is worthy of the greatest care and consideration. It is surprising that so little attention is given to vocal hygiene, when it is remembered that a serious weakness or affection of the throat may disqualify a speaker for important work. The delicate and intricate machinery of the vocal apparatus renders it peculiarly susceptible to misuse or exposure. The common defects of nasality, throatiness, and harshness, are due to wrong and careless use of the speaking—instrument.

In the training of the public speaker the first step is to bring the breathing apparatus under proper control. That is to say, the speaker must accustom himself, through careful practise, to use the abdominal method of breathing, and to keep his throat free from the strain to which it is commonly subjected. This form of breathing is not difficult to acquire, since it simply means that

向外鼓,呼气时肚子收缩。没有必要再提醒讲话人在不讲话时就只用鼻子呼吸。而讲话时,一定要完全控制好呼吸以便使其完全转变成声音。

“慢性咽炎” 就是嗓子运用不恰当或说话时声嘶力竭造成的。有时牧师热切的态度致使他讲话时用力“抓住”每一词,而不是把喉咙当成一条通道让声音轻松自如地从中流泻出来。许多讲话人为了能够让远处的听众听到自己的讲话，就提高嗓门儿大声喊话，忘记了最关键的是发音清楚准确。讲话时一直高声大嗓或者嘴张得不到位也会使嗓子感到难受。大多数咽喉上的毛病差不多都是由于缺乏正确的演讲训练造成的。要想让嗓子和喉咙保持正常,每天都应进行正规的训练,哪怕只训练 10 分钟也行。学习一些演员的做法也许会颇有裨益,那些演员白天在干其他事情的时候,偶尔也哼一会儿嗓子，以此来保持悦耳洪亮的嗓音。

当嗓子嘶哑或不响亮时，那便是生理在及时提醒你它需要休息和放松。如果在这种情况下仍然继续发表演讲,常会出现很大的危险,有时甚至

during inhalation the abdomen is expanded, and during exhalation it is contracted. It should be no longer necessary to warn the speaker to breathe exclusively through the nose when not actually using the voice. While speaking he must so completely control the breath that not a particle of it can escape without giving up its equivalent in sound.

"Clergyman's sore throat" is the result of improper use or overstraining of the voice. Sometimes the earnestness of the preacher causes him to "clutch" each word with the vocal muscles, instead of using the throat as an open channel through which the voice may flow with ease and freedom. Many speakers, in an endeavor to be heard at a great distance, employ too loud a tone, forgetting that the essential thing is a clear and distinct articulation. To speak continuously in high pitch, or through half-closed teeth, almost invariably causes distress of throat. Most throat troubles may be set down to a lack of proper elocutionary training. To keep the voice and throat in order there should be regular daily practise, if only for ten minutes. The example might profitably be followed of certain actors who make a practise of humming occasionally during the day while engaged in other duties, as a means of keeping the voice musical and resonant.

When the throat becomes husky or weak it is a timely warning from nature that it needs rest and relaxation. To continue to engage in public speaking under these circumstances is often

造成完全失声。一个简单的办法是在患重感冒或喉咙因其他原因发炎时，就不要再说话。紧张、焦虑或过大的精神压力可能会造成嗓音出毛病。这时，最好让嗓子休息一下，同时在冷水里滴点醋或科隆香水轻轻地漱漱喉咙。

演讲者刚刚结束演讲后，不要立即与他人没完没了地攀谈。走出演讲厅突然来到户外，讲话人应该闭紧自己的嘴巴。讲话人总的身体状况与其话音的力度和清晰度有很大关系。每天洗个凉水澡或者至少是用海绵蘸水擦擦全身，这不仅能够强身健体，还可以大大改善喉部和腹部的肌肉状况。从“浴盆”出来后，用毛巾和双手使劲搓搓身体，全身都会感到很有活力。

人们时常问起吸烟是否对咽喉有害，毫无疑问，权威的意见以及人们的经验都支持戒烟。任何一个曾经在烟雾缭绕的屋子里说过半小时或半个多小时话的人都知道那会让敏感的咽喉感到很难受。因此，经常吸入烟雾显然更会直接引发黏膜发炎。

演讲者的饮食要合理调节，切忌膳食过热或

attended with great danger, resulting sometimes in total loss of voice. It is economy in the end to discontinue the use of the voice when there is a serious cold or the throat is otherwise affected. Nervousness, anxiety, or unusual mental exertion may cause a vocal breakdown. For this condition rest is recommended, together with gentle massaging of the throat with cold water mixed with a little vinegar or *eau de Cologne.*

A public speaker should not engage in protracted conversation immediately after a speech. The sudden transition from an auditorium to the outer air should remind the speaker to keep his mouth securely closed. The general physical condition of the speaker has much to do with the vigor and clearness of his voice. A daily plunge into cold water, or at least a sponging of the entire surface of the body, besides being a tonic luxury, greatly invigorates the throat and abdominal muscles. After the "tub" a vigorous rubbing with towel and hands should produce a glow.

To the frequent question whether smoking is injurious to the throat, it is safe to say that the weight of authority and experience favors abstinence. Any one who has spoken for half an hour or more in a smoke-clouded room, knows the distressing effect it has had upon the sensitive lining of the throat. It must be obvious, therefore, that the constant inhaling of smoke must even more directly irritate the mucous membrane.

The diet of the public speaker should be reasonably moderate, and the extremes of hot and

过冷。最好不要喝冰水饮料。许多口服药剂和含片对咽喉肯定有害。如果嗓子总是干涩，喝点甘油或蜂蜜丸通常会缓解这种症状。莫雷尔·麦肯齐医生是英国杰出的咽喉专家，他认为酒对咽喉有害，他还坚持认为“即使是调得比较淡的酒也会使娇嫩的咽喉组织处于充血状态，而这很容易让咽喉因受凉或其他原因而发炎。”

千万不要认为喉咙特别娇气。适当地让它经受锻炼会使它变得坚韧，只要不过分，这么做是有好处的。除非是在特殊的情况下，不要用围巾把喉部裹起来，否则它会变得特别敏感，而且扭头时还会增加感冒的危险。

一位杰出的内科医生确信日常最好的漱口剂莫过于温水中放点盐。每天一早一晚都要用这种漱口剂保养喉咙。如果喉部黏膜有发炎的迹象，可用三等分的双氧水、金缕梅酊和水制成的溶剂漱口，其效果也很不错。除非在医生的直接指导下，否则不要用鼻子吸任何药物，因为那会导致耳聋。

许多演说家和歌手都喜欢用自己的偏方来改善嗓音。这些偏方五花八门而且很有趣，有热牛奶、茶水、咖啡、香槟酒、生鸡蛋、柠檬水、苹果、葡

cold avoided. The use of ice–water is to be discouraged. Many drugs and lozenges are positively injurious to the throat. For habitual dryness of throat a glycerine or honey tablet will usually obviate the trouble. Dr. Morell Mackenzie, the eminent English throat specialist, condemns the use of alcohol as pernicious, and affirms that "even in a comparatively mild form it keeps the delicate tissues in a state of congestion which makes them particularly liable to inflammation from cold or other causes."

It must not be assumed that the throat is to be pampered. A reasonable amount of exposure will harden it and to this extent is desirable. To muffle the throat with a scarf, unless demanded by special conditions, may make it unduly sensitive and increase the danger of taking cold when the head is turned from side to side.

A leading physician confirms the opinion that the best gargle for daily use is that of warm water and salt. This should be used every night and morning to cleanse and invigorate the throat. Where there is a tendency to catarrh a solution made of peroxide of hydrogen, witch–hazel, and water, in equal parts, will prove efficacious. Nothing should be snuffed up the nose except under the direction of a physician, lest it cause deafness.

Many speakers and singers have a favorite nostrum for improving the voice. The long and amusing list includes hot milk, tea, coffee, champagne, raw eggs, lemonade, apples, raisins,—

萄干，甚至还有沙丁鱼！如果进餐的时间刚好在演说之前，应该只吃七八分饱。几乎毋庸赘述，严重的喉部疾病，诸如扁桃体肿大、悬雍垂展长和喉鼻出现赘生物都是应该由专科医生解决的问题。

如果可能的话，演讲人要提前对他首次进行演讲的礼堂的拢音效果做一下检测。一个好办法就是让自己的一位朋友坐在礼堂或教堂的后面，然后对演讲人声音的质量和穿透力发表意见。演说人很难对自己的声音做出判断，因为他的声音不仅从外部而且通过耳咽管又经喉部和头部的振动部位调节后才传递给自己。演讲者所听到的自己的声音绝对跟别人所听到的不同。

也许没有什么其他方式比一直用同一种音调把话没完没了地讲下去更让嗓子感到疲惫的了。讲话人应该明智地交替使用两个声区。这就是“胸部”声区，声带在其中全程振动，音质的大部分特点也源于胸腔；再就是“头部”声区，声带在其中只是部分振动，音质通过面部、嘴和头的共振作用得到强化。前一种声区因音质圆润有时被称为“响”声 ，主要用于尊敬，庄严和崇高的言辞。

头部声区用于日常谈话，也是演讲风格的基

and sardines! A good rule is to eat sparingly if the meal is taken just before speaking. It need hardly be said that serious vocal defects, such as enlarged tonsils, elongated uvula, and abnormal growths in the throat and nose are subjects for the specialist.

Whenever possible a speaker should test beforehand the acoustic properties of the auditorium in which he is to speak for the first time. A helpful plan is to have a friend seat himself at the back of the hall or church, and give his opinion of the quality and projecting power of the speaker's voice. It is difficult to judge one's own voice because it is conveyed to him not only from the outside but also through the Eustachian tube and modified by the vibratory parts of the throat and head. A speaker never hears his own voice as it is heard by another.

Nothing, perhaps, is so taxing to the throat as long-continued speaking in one quality of tone. There are two distinct registers which should be judiciously alternated by the speaker. These are the "chest" register, in which the vocal cords vibrate their whole length, and the quality of tone derives most of its character from the chest cavity; and the "head" register, in which the vocal cords vibrate only in part, and the quality of tone is reenforced by the resonators of the face, mouth, and head. The first of these registers is sometimes called the "orotund" voice from its quality of roundness, and is employed principally in language of reverence, sublimity, and grandeur.

The head tone is the voice of ordinary conversation and should form the basis of the

础。

任何要在公开场合讲话的人都不应该因为嗓音条件有限而灰心丧气。许多出众的演说家起初也在这方面存在明显的不足，但他们把这些不足化作了更高追求的动力。一位优秀的演说家会通过十分清晰的吐字来弥补嗓音的不够洪亮，而另一位优秀的演说家则可能通过娴熟的语调变换来抵消听起来令人不悦的低沉的声音。

以下是一些易于记住的建议：

1. 演讲前要让嗓子休息一到两个小时。

2. 早晚用盐水漱洗喉咙。

3. 绝不要声嘶力竭地说话。

4. 避免参与伤及嗓子的一切活动，如没完没了的交谈，在嘈杂喧闹的环境里不得不大声讲话，或者在阴冷潮湿的环境里讲话。

5. 经常进行深呼吸锻炼使其成为一种自然而然的习惯。

6. 多去户外活动。

7. 每天哼几句小曲儿。

8. 重感冒或喉咙有其他炎症时，不要做公开演讲。

9. 做过演讲后，要立刻让嗓子和身体得到休息。

public-speaking style.

No one who has to speak in public should be discouraged because of limited vocal resources. Many of the foremost orators began with marked disadvantages in this respect, but made these shortcomings an incentive to higher effort. One well-known speaker makes up for lack of vocal power by extreme distinctness of enunciation, while another offsets an unpleasantly heavy quality of voice by skilful modulation.

A few easily remembered suggestions are:

1.Rest the voice for an hour or two before speaking in public.

2.Gargle the throat night and morning with salt and water.

3.Never force the voice.

4.Avoid all occasions that strain the voice, such as prolonged conversation, speaking against noise, or in cold and damp air.

5.Practise deep breathing until it becomes an unconscious habit.

6.Favor an outdoor life.

7.Hum or sing a little every day.

8.Discontinue public speaking when there is a severe cold or other affection of the throat.

9.Rest the voice and body immediately after speaking in public.

15.

演讲者的禁忌

切忌大喊大叫。
切忌信口开河。
切忌烦躁不安。
切忌阿谀逢迎。
切忌高谈阔论。
切忌油嘴滑舌。
切忌支支吾吾。
切忌带有鼻音。
切忌用辩解的语气讲话。
切忌主观臆断。
切忌言辞粗俗。
切忌惹人反感。
切忌姿态不雅。
切忌蛮横粗暴。
切忌人身攻击。
切忌言语“滑稽”。
切忌装腔作势。
切忌声音单调。

15.

Don´ts for Public Speakers

Don´t rant.
Don´t prate.
Don´t fidget.
Don´t flatter.
Don´t declaim.
Don´t be glib.
Don´t hesitate.
Don´t be nasal.
Don´t apologize.
Don´t dogmatize.
Don´t be slangy.
Don´t antagonize.
Don´t be awkward.
Don´t be violent.
Don´t be personal.
Don´t be "funny."
Don´t attitudinize.
Don´t be monotonous.

切忌语速过快。
切忌晃动身体。
切忌唠唠叨叨。
切忌哼哼哈哈。
切忌自卖自夸。
切忌手势幅度太大。
切忌在台上踱来踱去。
切忌频繁清嗓子。
切忌“得意地指指点点”。
切忌叙述长故事。
切忌踮起脚尖。
切忌曲解词义。
切忌站得如同泥塑木雕。
切忌对着天花板演讲。
切忌调门儿太高。
切忌事事强调。
切忌边讲话边喝水。
切忌使听众感到疲劳。
切忌演讲超时。
切忌没话找话。
切忌离题万里。
切忌边讲话边摸弄衣服。
切忌像咬着牙似的说话。
切忌手抵臀部。
切忌演讲完毕时当停不停。

Don´t speak rapidly.
Don´t sway your body.
Don´t be long–winded.
Don´t "hem" and "haw".
Don´t praise yourself.
Don´t overgesticulate.
Don´t pace the platform.
Don´t clear your throat.
Don´t "point with pride".
Don´t tell a long story.
Don´t rise on your toes.
Don´t distort your words.
Don´t stand like a statue.
Don´t address the ceiling.
Don´t speak in a high key.
Don´t emphasize everything.
Don´t drink while speaking.
Don´t fatigue your audience.
Don´t exceed your time limit.
Don´t talk for talking´s sake.
Don´t wander from your subject.
Don´t fumble with your clothes.
Don´t speak through closed teeth.
Don´t put your hands on your hips.
Don´t fail to stop when you have ended.

16.

演讲者谨记

准备充分。

开场平缓。

虚心谦和。

条理清晰。

面向全场听众。

始终彬彬有礼。

删繁就简。

提高思维的敏捷性。

在说理方法上不露痕迹。

言语审慎清楚。

相信自己。

直视听众。

开门见山。

多用沉稳的语调。

言辞考究。

有理有据。

严肃认真。

停顿适当。

16.

Do's for Public Speakers

Be prepared.
Begin slowly.
Be modest.
Speak distinctly.
Address all your hearers.
Be uniformly courteous.
Prune your sentences.
Cultivate mental alertness.
Conceal your method.
Be scrupulously clear.
Feel sure of yourself.
Look your audience in the eyes.
Be direct.
Favor your deep tones.
Speak deliberately.
Get to your facts.
Be earnest.
Observe your pauses.

言行一致。

自然大方。

话语流畅。

运用腹腔共鸣。

风趣幽默。

用随和的交谈方式。

化敌为友。

充满激情。

逻辑性强。

头脑冷静。

细心周到。

吐字口形到位。

话语掷地有声。

感情真挚。

简洁明了。

随机应变。

结尾干脆。

Suit the action to the word.
Be yourself at your best.
Speak fluently.
Use your abdominal muscles.
Make yourself interesting.
Be conversational.
Conciliate your opponent.
Rouse yourself.
Be logical.
Have your wits about you.
Be considerate.
Open your mouth.
Speak authoritatively.
Cultivate sincerity.
Cultivate brevity.
Cultivate tact.
End swiftly.

17.

演讲者注意要点

演讲者要尽量避免下面这些陈词滥调：

在此发言，本人感到诚惶诚恐……
敝人实在不习惯在公共场所讲话。
感谢命运眷顾，……
我深感责任重大。
归根结底……
我深受鼓舞才敢抛砖引玉……
我很自豪地指出……
另一方面（作手势）……
我坚信……
舆论认为……
如果那样的话……
我不会耽搁你们太久。
因为天色渐晚……
相信我，……
我们不无忧虑地看到……
正如我将告诉你们的一样……

17.

Points for Speakers

As far as possible avoid the following hackneyed phrases:

I rise with diffidence
Unaccustomed as I am to public speaking
By a happy stroke of fate
It becomes my painful duty
In the last analysis
I am encouraged to go on
I point with pride
On the other hand (with gesture)
I hold
The vox populi
Be that as it may
I shall not detain you
As the hour is growing late
Believe me
We view with alarm
As I was about to tell you

这是我人生中最高兴的一天。

本人有幸……

我不再赘述。

妍媸难辨……

我只能暗示……

无可奉告。

我无言以对。

事实是……

我认为……

这很难定夺。

恐怕……

我只能说……

我不会强加于人。

我绝不会……

就如凤凰涅槃一般,……

啊!

我还能再说什么呢?

在这夜幕降临的时分……

毋庸赘言……

机不可失……

请注意,那是因为……

我已经占用了太多的时间。

此事说来话长。

回忆童年,……

我们可以想象……

我既没有时间也没有能力……

不,亲爱的朋友们。

The happiest day of my life
It falls to my lot
I can say no more
In the fluff and bloom
I can only hint
I can say nothing
I cannot find words
The fact is
To my mind
I cannot sufficiently do justice
I fear
All I can say is
I shall not inflict a speech on you
Far be it from me
Rise phoenix–like from his ashes
But alas!
What more can I say?
At this late period of the evening
It is hardly necessary to say
I cannot allow the opportunity to pass
For, mark you
I have already taken up too much time
I might talk to you for hours
Looking back upon my childhood
We can imagine the scene
I haven't the time nor ability
Ah, no, dear friends

我最后只说一句……

最后……

我必须得结束了。

我的演讲到此结束。

One more word and I have done
I will now conclude
I really must stop
I have done.

18.

《圣经》论演讲

忠言力量大！

凡事皆有时，择时沉默，择时进言。

上帝啊，请严管吾嘴，慎开吾口。

出言有教益，开口无秽语。

善于听，慢于言，谨于怒。

言必优雅生动，而后方与人相谈。

交谈不可无礼。

抛却所有尖刻、气恼、愤怒、聒噪之词及恶言恶语。

适时抚慰意气消沉之人。

让我所言所想，为上帝——我的力量源泉、我的救世主所容。

18.

The Bible on Speech

How forcible are right words!

To every thing there is a season, a time to keep silence, and a time to speak.

Set a watch, O Lord, before my mouth; keep the door of my lips.

Let no corrupt communication proceed out of your mouth, but that which is good to the use of edifying.

Be swift to hear, slow to speak, slow to wrath.

Let your speech be always with grace, seasoned with salt, that ye may know how ye ought to answer every man.

Be ye holy in all manner of conversation.

Let all bitterness, and wrath, and anger, and clamor, and evil speaking, be put away from you.

Know how to speak a word in season to him that is weary.

Let the words of my mouth, and the meditation of my heart, be acceptable in Thy sight, O Lord, my strength, and my redeemer.

19.

关于谈话的深思妙想

天赋、学识甚至机智、雄辩都不足以成就一位出色的谈话者，这些或多或少都必须在某种程度上加上积极面对生活的才能。积极的生活态度对口才的提高所起的作用并不亚于智力、气质、情感、心魄，或许比那几种心智天赋所起的作用更大。“拿破仑有些话与他那些著名的战役一样永存于史册。马丁·路德的《漫谈录》与他焚烧教皇诏书的那把火一样发散着耀眼的光辉”。而口才出色的恺撒、西塞罗、地米斯托克利、培根勋爵、塞尔登、塔列朗以及我们本国的艾伦·伯尔、杰弗逊、韦伯斯特和乔特在某种程度上都可以说是实干家。在一次盛大的晚宴上，沃尔特·司各特爵士说他认为律师比主教更善于辞令，而主教比智者在谈话上更胜一筹。几乎所有伟大的雄辩家都是善谈者，唯独查塔姆勋爵（威廉·皮特）是个例外。他在上议院提出对糖征收附加税时曾语惊四座，私底下他却平淡无奇。皮特和福克斯的谈话字字珠玑。柏克的言论虽然看似散漫，却极其深刻华丽，极具引

19.

Thoughts on Talking

To make a good talker, genius and learning, even wit and eloquence, are insufficient; to these, in all or in part, must be added in some degree the talents of active life. The character has as much to do with colloquial power as has the intellect; the temperament, feelings, and animal spirits, even more, perhaps, than the mental gifts. "Napoleon said things which tell in history like his battles. Luther's Table-Talk glows with the fire that burnt the Pope's bull." Caesar, Cicero, Themistocles, Lord Bacon, Selden, Talleyrand, and, in our own country, Aaron Burr, Jefferson, Webster, and Choate, were all, more or less, men of action. Sir Walter Scott tells us that, at a great dinner party, he thought the lawyers beat the Bishops as talkers, and the Bishops the wits. Nearly all great orators have been fine talkers. Lord Chatham, who could electrify the House of Lords by pronouncing the word "Sugar", but who in private was but commonplace, was an exception; but the conversation of Pitt and Fox was brilliant and fascinating,—that of Burke, rambling, but splendid,

导力。后者是“文学俱乐部”中唯一一位在高谈阔论时能与约翰逊匹敌的人。约翰逊博士承认柏克是一位值得较量的劲敌。一次,因生病而憔悴不堪的约翰逊说:“我得全力以赴才能不被柏克那家伙比下去。若是现在见到他,那真会要了我的命。”又有一次,他说:“先生,即便你在街上为躲避一群牛而闪避路边,恰好与他在那里第一次碰面共处了短短的 5 分钟,他说话的方式也足以令你在分别时说:‘他真是个不一般的人’。由此看来,柏克的确是个不寻常的人。”提到某位能言善辩者时,作家奥利弗·哥尔德斯密斯问道:“他能像柏克一样不露痕迹地巧妙进入话题吗?”福克斯说他从柏克的谈话中获得的政治信息远远超过了他从书本、科学以及处世经验中所得到的政治信息的总和。穆尔也说过同样赞扬的话。他说柏克讲话就像罗马凯旋的过程一样,每一步都显示出力量和财富,偶尔交织着低俗的笑话和傲慢的进行曲,但始终闪耀着旁征博引、知识渊博的光彩。

——马修斯

总的来说,文人谈话的缺陷在于它太不依不饶,紧扣主题,从不放松。它更像一场战役而不是小战斗,把本该快乐的事弄得很辛苦。这种缺陷的造成大概是迫不得已,是由于有意追求更常见的

rich and instructive, beyond description. The latter was the only man in the famous "Literary Club" who could cope with Johnson. The Doctor confessed that in Burke he had a foeman worthy of his steel. On one occasion, when debilitated by sickness, he said: "That fellow calls forth all my powers. Were I to see Burke now, it would kill me." At another time he said: "Burke, sir, is such a man that, if you met him for the first time in the street, where you were stopped by a drove of oxen, and you and he stepped aside to take shelter but for five minutes, he'd talk to you in such a manner, that when you parted you'd say—'This is an extraordinary man.'" "Can he wind into a subject like a serpent, as Burke does?" asked Goldsmith of a certain talker. Fox said that he had derived more political information from Burke's conversation alone than from books, science, and all his worldly experience put together. Moore finely says of the same conversation, that it must have been like the procession of a Roman triumph, exhibiting power and riches at every step, occasionally mingling the low Fescennine jest with the lofty music of the march, but glittering all over with the spoils of a ransacked world.

—Mathews.

The fault of literary conversation in general is its too great tenaciousness. It fastens upon a subject, and will not let it go. It resembles a battle rather than a skirmish, and makes a toil of a pleasure. Perhaps it does this from necessity, from a

文雅和娱乐戏谑的能力，是想面面俱到、想把出现的问题都令人愉快地掩饰起来。那些有失败名声的人太想大放异彩，却难以心满意足。一位智者曾说："一个人要想在谈话中脱颖而出，不能总一味说好的事情：说一件好事意味着必须说很多坏的东西和更多无关紧要的东西。"只有大放异彩的愿望而没有真才实学通常会使人张不开口——对张不开口的担忧反而使人哑口无言。

一位习惯于用合乎逻辑的观点去看困难问题并逐步彻底解决它的作家，可能缺乏老于世故的人通常所拥有的敏捷和悠闲。后者习惯听取各种意见，对不同问题有不同观点。他们所关心的只是别让眼前闲暇的时光溜掉。一位作家在研究一个特定问题时的表现是：他阅读、查询、仔细思考，不愿与他人共同探讨，不愿给出暗示或提出异议，于是他或者保持沉默、忧心忡忡、心有不甘，或者推翻重来、善始善终。因为他完全把任务放在了自己肩上。他可能被认为在这个问题上懂得比别人多，或者他想表明别人根本不懂得这个问题。文坛新

consciousness of wanting the more familiar graces, the power to sport and trifle, to touch lightly and adorn agreeably, every view or turn of a question *en passant*, as it arises. Those who have a reputation to lose are too ambitious of shining, to please. "To excel in conversation," said an ingenious man, "one must not be always striving to say good things: to say one good thing, one must say many bad, and more indifferent ones." This desire to shine without the means at hand, often makes men silent:—

The fear of being silent strikes us dumb.

A writer who has been accustomed to take a connected view of a difficult question and to work it out gradually in all its bearings, may be very deficient in that quickness and ease which men of the world, who are in the habit of hearing a variety of opinions, who pick up an observation on one subject, and another on another, and who care about none any further than the passing away of an idle hour, usually acquire. An author has studied a particular point—he has read, he has inquired, he has thought a great deal upon it: he is not contented to take it up casually in common with others, to throw out a hint, to propose an objection: he will either remain silent, uneasy, and dissatisfied, or he will begin at the beginning, and go through with it to the end. He is for taking the whole responsibility upon himself. He would be thought to understand the subject better than others, or indeed would show that nobody else knows anything about it. There are always three or

手在其文字生涯的开始阶段总会有几次不现实的幻想，幻想他能启迪每个伙伴，打败所有的对手。但这种空想好斗的脾性终将被矫正，当他深入社会之后，他会发现，除此之外，自己还有一些其他的观念以及自以为是的想法需要矫正。当这种不知天高地厚的态度逐渐消失时，则会渐渐出现文雅老练的变化，文人的谈话也就会变得风趣而有启发性。老于世故的人没有固定的原则，也没有基本的思想，唯独学者执著于目标，心里总装着某种理论，他们将一切都跟理论挂上钩，而这些理论时常是大家认可的常识。通过与社会融合，他们抛弃了僵化的风格和不切实际、得罪人的个性，保留下见解的深度和连贯性，那么他们本身的经历将比他们写的书更有可学之处。

——黑兹利特

有那么一些人，他们彬彬有礼，因此一般不会打断你的话，但是那彬彬有礼的样子中却透露着极度的不耐烦，并且一直等候着你把话讲完——这也同样很糟糕。这是因为他们心中出现了自己的想法，并且急于表达出来。同时，他们根本不注意事物的发展，他们把想象力完全集中在心中已有的观念上，唯恐这些观念会从记忆中悄悄溜走，结果他们就限制了自己的创造力，不然的话那创

four points on which the literary novice at his first outset in life fancies he can enlighten every company, and bear down all opposition: but he is cured of this quixotic and pugnacious spirit, as he goes more into the world, where he finds that there are other opinions and other pretensions to be adjusted besides his own. When this asperity wears off, and a certain scholastic precocity is mellowed down, the conversation of men of letters becomes both interesting and instructive. Men of the world have no fixed principles, no groundwork of thought: mere scholars have too much an object, a theory always in view, to which they wrest everything, and not unfrequently, common sense itself. By mixing with society, they rub off their hardness of manner, and impracticable, offensive singularity, while they retain a greater depth and coherence of understanding. There is more to be learnt from them than from their books.

—Hazlitt

There are some people whose good manners will not suffer them to interrupt you, but, what is almost as bad, will discover abundance of impatience, and lie upon the watch until you have done, because they have started something in their own thoughts, which they long to be delivered of. Meantime, they are so far from regarding what passes, that their imaginations are wholly turned upon what they have in reserve, for fear it should slip out of their memory; and thus they confine

造力可能会创造出上百种好东西，而且那创造力本来是可以更自然地为其所用的。

有一种所谓的熟不拘礼，一些人常在与至交好友相处时这么做，并且推而广之，在与一般人谈话时也是如此，认为这不过是坦率或幽默的表现。这种熟不拘礼在我们北方的环境中则是危险的做法。因为在这里我们那点端庄与礼貌完全是艺术性的装饰，随时可能演变为粗野。古罗马人用熟不拘礼的话戏弄奴隶，在普劳图斯的剧本中就有不少这样的例子。大概是克伦威尔将它介绍给了我们。克伦威尔喜欢人们的粗俗话语，于是便把口无遮拦的习惯变成了高雅的消遣。我听说过许多这方面的事例。考虑到一切都黑白颠倒了，这也就是合情合理的了，绅士们会因为一句无足轻重的话说得不当就要决斗，其实，决斗只是用来嘲笑极端好面子的表现的另一种极端行为。

有的人非常善于讲故事，并且脑子里有大量的存货，需要时在任何场合都能拿出来一段。想想现在人们的谈话已经如此粗俗，善于讲故事也就不是什么完全不登大雅之堂的才能了。但是，它有两个不可避免的弊端，即频繁重复和所储存的故事会很快竭尽。因此无论是谁自视有此才能，都需要有很好的记忆力，并且不断改变交际圈子，才有

their invention, which might otherwise range over a hundred things full as good, and that might be much more naturally introduced.

There is a sort of rude familiarity, which some people, by practising among their intimates, have introduced into their general conversation, and would have it pass for innocent freedom or humor; which is a dangerous experiment in our northern climate, where all the little decorum and politeness we have are purely forced by art, and are so ready to lapse into barbarity. This, among the Romans, was the raillery of slaves, of which we have many instances in Plautus. It seems to have been introduced among us by Cromwell, who, by preferring the scum of the people, made it a court entertainment, of which I have heard many particulars; and, considering all things were turned upside down, it was reasonable and judicious; although it was a piece of policy found out to ridicule a point of honor in the other extreme, when the smallest word misplaced among gentlemen ended in a duel.

There are some men excellent at telling a story, and provided with a plentiful stock of them, which they can draw out upon occasion in all companies, and, considering how low conversation runs now among us, it is not altogether a contemptible talent; however, it is subject to two unavoidable defects, frequent repetition, and being soon exhausted; so, that, whoever values this gift in himself, has need of a good memory, and ought frequently to shift his company, that he may not

可能不觉得自己储备不足。而且由于拥有这种能力的人几乎没有其他的谈资，也就只能依靠这最主要的储备了。

——斯威夫特

交谈中精神上的最高条件是我们所说的圆通。之所以说“条件”，是因为无法判断它是否是一种单独的特质，或者很可能那是才思敏捷和深切同情的结合。显然这是一种智力特质，与其他特点不同，这种能力即使不能真正习得，也能通过长期的社会历练而大大提高。跟所有社交方面的特长一样，圆通的特长也几乎是某些人的天赋，而其他人费尽辛劳也无法拥有。就像台球、射击、板球等一切既需要脑力又需要体力的技能一样，许多人永远都只是一般水平。不过，即便是有天赋的人也必须练习，只有付出了艰苦努力才能真正出类拔萃。艺术家也是如此。音乐和绘画才能并非人人可得，甚至对这些艺术的正确的评论也离不开天赋才能；然而，经常到高级画廊里和高雅音乐会上去学习，长期与艺术家交往也有助于使资质平庸的人成为优秀的技艺评判者。

圆通的才能即是准确、迅速的判断能力，它能判断出交际是否得体融洽，它同样也是一种微妙

discover the weakness of his fund; for those who are thus endued have seldom any other revenue, but live upon the main stock.

—Swift

The highest and best of all the moral conditions for conversation is what we call tact. I say a condition, for it is very doubtful whether it can be called a single and separate quality; more probably it is a combination of intellectual quickness with lively sympathy. But so clearly is it an intellectual quality, that of all others it can be greatly improved, if not actually acquired, by long experience in society. Like all social excellences it is almost given as a present to some people, while others with all possible labor never acquire it. As in billiard-playing, shooting, cricket, and all these other facilities which are partly mental and partly physical, many never can pass a certain point of mediocrity; but still even those who have the talent must practise it, and only become really distinguished after hard work. So it is in art. Music and painting are not to be attained by the crowd. Not even the just criticism of these arts is attainable without certain natural gifts; but a great deal of practice in good galleries and at good concerts, and years spent among artists, will do much to make even moderately-endowed people sound judges of excellence.

Tact, which is the sure and quick judgment of what is suitable and agreeable in society, is likewise one of those delicate and subtle qualities or a

精细的特质或几种特质的结合，它难以定义，因此没有固定的规律可以教授。有的人因为有同情心而获得；有的人因天生才智获得；有的人因头脑冷静获得；还有的人通过细心地观察邻里之人的过失获得。它的名称显示出，这是在社会交往中所表现出的机敏，是善于察言观色，能够从脸上的表情中看出那里掠过的一抹阴云，也能观察出那里是否有想把心事与人分享的欲望。这种圆通当然不仅能用于交谈。它最大的作用莫过于创造社交的良好环境，选择情投意合的伙伴，找出并推荐愉快的话题，排除一切干扰因素，使交谈的人不会遇上一点儿麻烦，因为即便是微不足道的小麻烦也会破坏社交的气氛。

——马哈菲

在平时的生活中，我们经常听到有人提及被认为是当初精辟的谈话的标准，也常听人提起当初一些辞采动人的谈话者的大名；然而如果我们出于真诚，不带一丝厌世怀旧的心理，我们必须承认按照那样的标准谈话，没有哪次不是带来深深

combination of qualities which is not very easily defined, and therefore not teachable by fixed precepts. Some people attain it through sympathy; others through natural intelligence; others through a calm temper; others again by observing closely the mistakes of their neighbors. As its name implies, it is a sensitive touch in social matters, which feels small changes of temperature, and so guesses at changes of temper; which sees the passing cloud on the expression of one face, or the eagerness of another that desires to bring out something personal for others to enjoy. This quality of tact is of course applicable far beyond mere actual conversation. In nothing is it more useful than in preparing the right conditions for a pleasant society, in choosing the people who will be in mutual sympathy, in thinking over pleasant subjects of talk and suggesting them, in seeing that all disturbing conditions are kept out, and that the members who are to converse should be all without those small inconveniences which damage society so vastly out of proportion to their intrinsic importance.

—Mahaffy

In the course of our life we have heard much of what was reputed to be the select conversation of the day, and we have heard many of those who figured at the moment as effective talkers; yet, in mere sincerity,and without a vestige of misanthropic retrospect, we must say that never once has it happened to us to come away from any display of that nature without intense disappointment; and it

的失望的；并且在我们看来，哪次失败（原本是失望）都是不可避免的。因为突出的困难在于：几乎所有需要技巧的活动差不多都要求较量的双方有对等的实力。无知的人会认为一个有实力的辩手对付一个弱的对手是一种优势；然而，恰恰相反，那简直是毁了他；因为他只有通过对手实力相当的抗衡才能显示出自己的实力。一个出色的击剑手与新手比试只会乱了章法，不知所措。这种情况在球类比赛、在打羽毛球或跳舞时也会发生。一个没有实力的对手或搭档不仅不会使你大显身手，反而会让你陷入无助，感到沮丧。好啦，如果晚会的主讲者或发起者有幸棋逢对手，那么很有可能会出现一次精彩的“唇枪舌剑的交锋”——虽然即使在那种情况下也需要机会创造合适的话题；即使有合适的话题，在这场炫耀才智的决斗中，占优势的一方也难免有粗俗和庸医耍宝的感觉。另一方面，假设优秀的谈话者受到和其他客人一样的招待，他在众人面前也就不会显得矜持，那么他谈起话来必定会选择以下两种方式之一：要么谈

always appeared to us that this failure (which soon ceased to be a disappointment) was inevitable by a necessity of the case. For here lay the stress of the difficulty: almost all depends in most trials of skill upon the parity of those who are matched against each other. An ignorant person supposes that to an able disputant it must be an advantage to have a feeble opponent; whereas, on the contrary, it is ruin to him; for he can not display his own powers but through something of a corresponding power in the resistance of his antagonist. A brilliant fencer is lost and confounded in playing with a novice; and the same thing takes place in playing at ball, or battledore, or in dancing, where a powerless partner does not enable you to shine the more, but reduces you to mere helplessness, and takes the wind altogether out of your sails. Now, if by some rare good luck the great talker, the protagonist, of the evening has been provided with a commensurate second, it is just possible that something like a brilliant "passage of arms" may be the result,—though much even in that case will depend on the chances of the moment for furnishing a fortunate theme, and even then, amongst the superior part of the company, a feeling of deep vulgarity and of mountebank display is inseparable from such an ostentatious duel of wit. On the other hand, supposing your great talker to be received like any other visitor, and turned loose upon the company, then he must do one of two things: either he will talk upon *outre*

论怪诞的、连自己也忌讳的话题——这样一来，这位优秀的谈话者的形象就会无异于站在街边的高台上向路人推销野药的江湖郎中。要么他就会像普通人一样谈论普通话题——这样一来，周围的人出于习惯性的礼貌，不会像看怪物一样看他，而是赶紧迎合他的风格，于是谈话变得普普通通、波澜不惊；尽管优秀的谈话者也许会显得通情达理、很有教养，但是同时，很遗憾，那个杰出的谈话者因为离开了自己原有的水平而黯然失色。总之，让谈话大师感到进退两难的是：如果他打算在大家都满足于步枪的时候，试图发射大炮来炫耀自己，无疑他会给人留下深刻的印象，但代价是使自己与大家在情感上格格不入，像被雇来表演走绳索把戏的怪物一样整个晚上都形只影单。反之，如果他收敛起才能的锋芒也像别人一样满足于步枪，那么对我们来说他和其他没有那种才能的人又有何不同呢？

——德·昆西

在谈话时，有的人渴望别人赞扬他有驾驭各种辩论的才智，而不是有能明辨真理的能力；似乎值得赞扬的是知道可以说什么，而不是知道应该思考什么。有的人说起某些寻常的事或话题十分

subjects specially tabooed to his own private use,—in which case the great man has the air of a quack-doctor addressing a mob from a street stage; or else he will talk like ordinary people upon popular topics,—in which case the company, out of natural politeness, that they may not seem to be staring at him as a lion, will hasten to meet him in the same style, the conversation will become general, the great man will seem reasonable and well-bred, but at the same time, we grieve to say it, the great man will have been extinguished by being drawn off from his exclusive ground. The dilemma, in short, is this:—If the great talker attempts the plan of showing off by firing cannon-shot when everybody else is content with musketry, then undoubtedly he produces an impression, but at the expense of insulating himself from the sympathies of the company, and standing aloof as a sort of monster hired to play tricks of funambulism for the night. Yet, again, if he contents himself with a musket like other people, then for us, from whom he modestly hides his talents under a bushel, in what respect is he different from the man who has no such talent?

—De Quincey

Some, in their discourse, desire rather commendation of wit, in being able to hold all arguments, than of judgment, in discerning what is true; as if it were a praise to know what might be said, and not what should be thought. Some have certain commonplaces and themes wherein they are

在行，并且总是老一套，这种内容贫乏的老生常谈常令人厌烦，并且一被发现就会显得很可笑。谈话中最可敬的做法是引出话题，然后再平缓自然地使其转移到其他话题，就像有一个人领舞一样。谈话或演讲最好不要单调，可以寓论证于时事评论，寓道理于故事，寓观点于提问，寓激情于玩笑。完全可以说，使人疲倦或把事情扯太远都是愚蠢的做法。说到玩笑，有些东西是不可以拿来嘲弄的，具体说来有宗教、国家大事、伟人、别人的紧要事务、灾难；然而还是有人认为要是不语出惊人，不说些刺激、敏感的事就埋没了自己的才智。这样的心态是应该控制的；“小伙子哟，请少用鞭子，多拉缰绳”。（注： 原为拉丁文——译者注）此外，一般说来，人们还应该明白尖锐与尖刻的区别。善于挖苦对手的人在让人害怕他才智的同时，自己也会担心别人记恨。好问的人可以学到很多东西、同时让被请教之人获得满足，但要注意就别人的专长而问，给别人从回答中得到乐趣的机会，而自己则不断积累了知识；同时问题不要太难，因为只有善于装模作样的人才会回答太难的问题；还要确保给其他人留下发言的时间；一旦有什么话题可能会占据所有时间，就要想办法岔开话题，把别的

good, and want variety; which kind of poverty is for the most part tedious, and, when it is once perceived, ridiculous. The honorablest part of talk is to give the occasion; and again to moderate and pass to somewhat else; for then a man leads the dance. It is good in discourse, and speech of conversation, to vary, and intermingle speech of the present occasion with arguments, tales with reasons, asking of questions with telling of opinions, and jest with earnest; for it is a dull thing to tire, and, as we say now, to jade any thing too far. As for jest, there be certain things which ought to be privileged from it, namely, religion, matters of State, great persons, any man's present business of importance, and any case that deserveth pity; yet there be some that think their wits have been asleep, except they dart out somewhat that is piquant, and to the quick. That is a vein which would be bridled; *Parce, puer, stimulis, et fortius utere loris*. And, generally, men ought to find the difference between saltness and bitterness. Certainly, he that hath a satirical vein, as he maketh others afraid of his wit, so he had need be afraid of others' memory. He that questioneth much shall learn much, and content much, but especially if he apply his questions to the skill of the persons whom he asketh; for he shall give them occasion to please themselves in speaking, and himself shall continually gather knowledge; but let his questions not be troublesome, for that is fit for a poser; and let him be sure to leave other men their turns to speak; nay, if there be any that would reign and

话题介绍进来，就像乐师常对跳三步舞跳得太久的人所做的那样。如果有时别人认为你应当知道的事你装作不知道，那么下一次你本来就不知道的东西别人也会认为你是知道的。关于自己的事要少说、慎说。人们常常会轻蔑地说：“他一定是满腹经纶啊，一说起自己来就滔滔不绝。”只有在一种情况下可以欣然地顺便夸赞自己几句，那就是在夸赞别人的美德时，尤其是那种美德自己也在苦苦追求时。涉及别人的话少说，因为谈话应该是一片阔野，不应该针对任何个人。我认识英格兰西部的两位贵族，有一位喜欢嘲笑别人，但是却常在家里举行盛大的酒宴；另一位就问曾经去过前者家中做过客的人：“老实说，难道他在家里就不嘲笑别人或挖苦别人吗？”客人回答道：“这样的事情的确发生过。”发问的那位贵族老爷则说：“我早就料到他会毁了一次盛宴。”谨慎的话语比口才更有说服力；令人愉快的话比花言巧语更有用。没有良好的交流，一味娓娓而谈则难免显得拖沓沉闷；没有好的铺垫，机敏的回答或补充发言也会显得肤浅无力。就像野兽一样，那些被追赶时跑不快

take up all the time, let him find means to take them off, and to bring others on, as musicians use to do with those that dance too long galliards. If you dissemble sometimes your knowledge of that you are thought to know, you shall be thought, another time, to know that you know not. Speech of a man's self ought to be seldom, and well chosen. I knew one was wont to say in scorn, "He must needs be a wise man, he speaks so much of himself;" and there is but one case wherein a man may commend himself with good grace, and that is in commending virtue in another, especially if it be such a virtue whereunto himself pretendeth. Speech of touch towards others should be sparingly used; for discourse ought to be as a field, without coming home to any man. I knew two noblemen, of the west part of England, whereof the one was given to scoff, but kept ever royal cheer in his house; the other would ask of those that had been at the other's table, "Tell truly, was there never a flout or dry blow given?" To which the guest would answer, "Such and such a thing passed." The lord would say, "I thought he would mar a good dinner." Discretion of speech is more than eloquence; and to speak agreeably to him with whom we deal, is more than to speak in good words, or in good order. A good continued speech, without a good speech of interlocution, shows slowness; and a good reply, or second speech, without a good settled speech, showeth shallowness and weakness. As we see in beasts, that those that are weakest in the course, are yet

的动物，要善于灵活地转弯才能避开危险，野兔被猎狗追赶时就是如此。用太多的铺垫引出话题，令人乏味，但一点儿铺垫也没有就太直率了。

——培根

尽量少想自身的优点，目光绝不要总盯着自己的成就、影响、宏图大志、不菲业绩和追随者；最重要的是，尽量少说自己。过度的自爱很容易使我们在谈话时自吹自擂，就像干柴遇上烈火，一下子就能燃烧起来那样。除了向上帝忏悔自己的罪孽之外，只有职责需要我们介绍自己时，我们才张口谈这个危险的话题。此外，要格外警惕虚荣的人耍计谋把谈话引向他自己，以便获得赞赏或注意来满足自己贪婪的耳朵。即使人们主动称赞你，你也要警惕并反省，心中要找点儿隐秘的缘由向上帝谦卑地忏悔。想象一下如果那些只有你知、上帝知的事突然公诸于众，这些美妙的夸赞将变成什么。

——威尔伯福斯

说到有责任使别人感到愉快的问题，我们无

nimblest in the turn; as it is betwixt the greyhound and the hare. To use too many circumstances, ere one come to the matter, is wearisome; to use none at all, is blunt.

—Bacon

Think as little as possible about any good in yourself; turn your eyes resolutely from any view of your acquirement, your influence, your plan, your success, your following: above all, speak as little as possible about yourself. The inordinateness of our self-love makes speech about ourselves like the putting of the lighted torch to the dried wood which has been laid in order for the burning. Nothing but duty should open our lips upon this dangerous theme, except it be in humble confession of our sinfulness before our God. Again, be specially upon the watch against those little tricks by which the vain man seeks to bring round the conversation to himself, and gain the praise or notice which the thirsty ears drink in so greedily; and even if praise comes unsought, it is well, whilst men are uttering it, to guard yourself by thinking of some secret cause for humbling yourself inwardly to God; thinking into what these pleasant accents would be changed if all that is known to God, and even to yourself, stood suddenly revealed to man.

—Wilberforce

In speaking of the duty of pleasing others, it will not be necessary to dwell on the ordinary

需细说日常生活中应有的礼貌和基本的善良，更无需赘言这些东西无论多么细微都不会被有教养的人忽视……但是有一点我必须要提，因为我们大多数人都容易在这方面有所欠缺。那就是在理解那些职业、爱好或生活环境迥异于我们的人的兴趣和见解时，我们做得往往不到位……一般说来，凡是能跟别人交谈得起来的人都能有所收获。然而为获得这一利益，双方都必须有宽容的精神；每一方都必须愿意真诚地听对方讲话、愿意毫无偏见地回答对方的问题；任何一方都要尽力让对方愉快。我们都由于缺乏对不同社会阶层人们的习惯、观点和情感的了解，而有不小的损失。

——阿诺德博士

如果与人相处时你想获得别人的爱，请避免对周围的人妄加指责。任何社会里都有很多人擅自使用法官的权限。一个人很难与总是批评自己行为的人相处，即使那些批评是善意而正确的，那会像生活在显微镜下。而那些自命的法官，就像真法官那样，也常常把被自己评价的人像罪犯似的加以审问。

courtesies and lesser kindnesses of our daily living, any further than to observe that none of these things, however trifling, is beneath the notice of a good man, ... but I mention one thing, because I think that we are most of us apt to be rather deficient in it, and that is in the trying to suit ourselves to the tastes and views of persons whose professions or inclinations, or situation in life, differ widely from our own. ... As a general rule, no man can fall into conversation with another without being able to learn something valuable from him. But in order to get at this benefit there must be something of an accommodating spirit on both sides; each must be ready to hear candidly and to answer fairly; each must try to please the other. We all suffer from the want of acquaintance with the habits and opinions and feelings of different classes of society.

—Dr. Arnold

If you would be loved as a companion, avoid unnecessary criticism upon those with whom you live. The number of people who have taken out judges´ patents for themselves is very large in any society. Now it would be hard for a man to live with another who was always criticising his actions, even if it were kindly and just criticism. It would be like living between the glasses of a microscope. But these self–elected judges, like their prototypes, are very apt to have the persons they judge brought before them in the guise of culprits.

不要让熟不拘礼的放肆取代传统的礼貌。我们很多人习惯于像在背后说陌生人似的对生活在一起的人说一些放肆的话。然而，真正的礼貌往往在我们认为它是多余的时候恰恰最为重要。你可以对你的伙伴更多地说老实话，甚至说得更直白，但你对他们的礼貌应不啻于对待一个陌生人。

——赫尔普斯

生活中有很多悲伤都来源于一些琐事的积累。这些日复一日，年复一年不断积累的琐事有：一封不够礼貌的信，早餐时关于日程安排的一次争吵，进城路上熟人的粗鲁寒暄，有业务往来的另一公司不友好的举措，好事者多嘴传到耳边的恶意批评，下午茶时某人笑里藏刀的虚礼，孩子不听话，人际圈子中某人的轻视，一场过于激烈的争论。诸如此类的琐事数不胜数，但是细想起来没有一件是不可避免的，只要我们自己或我们的同仁多一丁点儿慈善之心，也没有哪一件是不可宽恕的。我们社交时的粗鲁，使人不快的行为，挑剔的评价，恶意的信件，带刺的的话语，都是蓄意刻薄的表现，都是性情不好的证明。

——约翰·沃森

Let not familiarity swallow up old courtesy. Many of us have a habit of saying to those with whom we live such things as we say about strangers behind their backs. There is no place, however, where real politeness is of more value than where we mostly think it would be superfluous. You may say more truth, or rather speak out more plainly to your associates, but not less courteously than to strangers.

—Helps

Much of the sorrow of life springs from the accumulation, day by day and year by year, of little trials—a letter written in less than courteous terms, a wrangle at the breakfast table over some arrangement of the day, the rudeness of an acquaintance on the way to the city, an unfriendly act on the part of another firm, a cruel criticism needlessly reported by some meddler, a feline amenity at afternoon tea, the disobedience of one of your children, a social slight by one of your circle, a controversy too hotly conducted. The trials within this class are innumerable, and consider, not one of them is inevitable, not one of them but might have been spared if we or our brother man had had a grain of kindliness. Our social insolences, our irritating manners, our censorious judgment, our venomous letters, our pin pricks in conversation, are all forms of deliberate unkindness, and are all evidences of an ill-conditioned nature.

—John Watson

如果为周围人创造快乐是我们的主要职责之一，那么毫无疑问暴躁的脾气则完全与这一职责相违背，并且阻碍了它的履行。因为除此之外，世界上能遇到的一切都不会带来那么频繁、那么剧烈、那么无谓的痛苦。因一句话而不悦，敏感的脾气；因有意无意的任何事生气，易怒的脾气；一触即发、蛮不讲理，暴躁的脾气；整天绷着脸、心中有怒气也一言不发，嫉妒或抑郁的脾气；自怨自艾，不知满足的脾气；对做过的事只看缺点，苛刻的脾气；无视是非、只为满足每一次心血来潮，任性的脾气；——要是能够总结出后果，即可看出它们对人们的心灵造成了多大的伤害！它们使多少人心生邪念，使多少祈祷被扼杀在口中，使多少真爱变成了仇恨！有时它们会使所有职责寸步难行！使日常生活痛苦不堪！它们残酷地扼杀了最温馨甜美的家庭幸福！其他过失造成的苦难通常更深切，更具灾难性，看起来更可怕；但是我坚信，把坏脾气造成的痛苦累积起来，一定会超过人们所承受的其他一切相互之间的伤害。

——坦普尔

If this be one of our chief duties—promoting the happiness of our neighbors—most certainly there is nothing which so entirely runs counter to it, and makes it impossible, as an undisciplined temper. For of all the things that are to be met with here on earth, there is nothing which can give such continual, such cutting, such useless pain. The touchy and sensitive temper, which takes offence at a word; the irritable temper, which finds offence in everything whether intended or not; the violent temper, which breaks through all bounds of reason when once roused; the jealous or sullen temper, which wears a cloud on the face all day, and never utters a word of complaint; the discontented temper, brooding over its own wrongs; the severe temper, which always looks at the worst side of whatever is done; the wilful temper, which overrides every scruple to gratify a whim,—what an amount of pain have these caused in the hearts of men, if we could but sum up their results! How many a soul have they stirred to evil impulses; how many a prayer have they stifled; how many an emotion of true affection have they turned to bitterness! How hard they sometimes make all duties! How painful they make all daily life! How they kill the sweetest and warmest of domestic charities! The misery caused by other sins is often much deeper and much keener, more disastrous, more terrible to the sight; but the accumulated pain caused by ill-temper must, I verily believe, if added together, outweigh all other pains that men have to bear from one another.

—Temple

诽谤是恶毒的——某人在某天下午把诽谤的话散布出来，随后它便在一连串熟人中迅速地流传，在他们所有人身上留下一滴毒药，还留下些许怀疑，或者不祥的沉默——“你没听说吗？”——“真是难以置信，但是——！”然后是沉默，同时摇摇头或耸耸肩，话虽然打住了，可那言外之意却比直接挑明更糟。你是否想过言语有覆水难收的天性？一旦说出，永难收回。多年以后，你会发现当初不经意的话语导致了某个人终生不快乐，或毁了一个家庭的平静。圣詹姆斯说得好：“如果你们当中有人看上去信仰虔诚，却管不住自己的舌头，那么他的信仰就是空的。”

——斯托普福德·布鲁克

沉默有三种：少言寡语的沉默很好，因为无节制的说东道西易导致邪恶；清心寡欲的沉默更佳，因为它有益于心灵的平和；但最佳的沉默出自不胡思乱想的沉默，因为它对于内心的平静至关重要，并且还能为形成良好的自制力和在其他方面的沉稳打下基础。

——居永夫人

我们的主谦逊、平静地接受这个村庄的断然拒绝，转身去往另一个村庄，他的例子也许对我们

Wicked is the slander which gossips away a character in an afternoon, and runs lightly over a whole series of acquaintances, leaving a drop of poison on them all, some suspicion, or some ominous silence—"Have you not heard?"—"No one would believe it, but—!" and then silence; while the shake of the head, or the shrug of the shoulders, finishes the sentence with a mute meaning worse than words. Do you ever think of the irrevocable nature of speech? The things you say are often said forever. You may find, years after your light word was spoken, that it has made a whole life unhappy, or ruined the peace of a household. It was well said by St. James, "If any man among you seem to be religious, and bridleth not his tongue, that man's religion is vain."

—Stopford Brooke

There are three kinds of silence. Silence from words is good, because inordinate speaking tends to evil. Silence, or rest from desires and passions, is still better, because it promotes quietness of spirit. But the best of all is silence from unnecessary and wandering thoughts, because that is essential to internal recollection, and because it lays a foundation for a proper regulation and silence in other respects.

—Madame Guyon

The example of our Lord, as He humbly and calmly takes the rebuff, and turns to go to another

平凡的日常生活中平常的处世方式有所启迪。我们不得不打交道的人在言行举止上常有让我们恼怒的小毛病；在我们看来有些事是丝毫不顾及他人的讨厌的任性妄为，于是我们会觉得无法跟能做出那种事情的人相处；有些错误我们认为是任何人都无权去犯的错误；谈话中有些话相当肤浅、或相当保守、或相当狭隘、或相当武断，它们足以令我们退缩或者让我们情不自禁地流露出冷酷邪恶的轻蔑——当然，在所有这些事情中，以及许多类似的其他事情中，我们的良心可能时刻准备着对我们说：我们其实有很多机会去效仿主高尚的谦逊和耐心。只要我们更谨慎地给那些人一些时间、不急于做出评判、相信他们过一会儿会更公正地看问题或者更明智地说话，那么我们将赢得并维系更多的友谊，我们将发现许多可以为他人效劳的机会，我们将吸取许多经验教训，纯洁无瑕的美丽心灵将充分地展现在我们面前。而如果我们任由自己妄想能迅速估量同胞的能力并改变他们的性格，那么我们必定会关上同情之门，会失去许多生活的趣味和工作的机会。

——佩吉特

人们挥霍浪费了那么多声音进行交谈，可取得的效果却微乎其微！也很少有敢于表现自己的

village, may help us in the ordinary ways of ordinary daily life. The little things that vex us in the manner or the words of those with whom we have to do; the things which seem to us so inconsiderate, or wilful, or annoying, that we think it impossible to get on with the people who are capable of them; the mistakes which no one, we say, has any right to make; the shallowness, or conventionality, or narrowness, or positiveness in talk which makes us wince and tempts us towards the cruelty and wickedness of scorn;—surely in all these things, and in many others like them, of which conscience may be ready enough to speak to most of us, there are really opportunities for thus following the example of our Saviour's great humility and patience. How many friendships we might win or keep, how many chances of serving others we might find, how many lessons we might learn, how much of unsuspected moral beauty might be disclosed around us, if only we were more careful to give people time, to stay judgment, to trust that they will see things more justly, speak of them more wisely, after a while. We are sure to go on closing doors of sympathy, and narrowing in the interests and opportunities of work around us, if we let ourselves imagine that we can quickly measure the capacities and sift the characters of our fellow-men.

—Paget

How much squandering there is of the voice! How little is there of the advantage that may come

同情和热诚的时候！人们自己常会轻易染上坏习惯。他们很害怕学校里的教育和训练，结果毕业后讲起话来往往显得缺少演讲技巧，其实也就是缺少教育。

父亲、母亲或家人温柔的声音多么美妙啊！把所有弦乐器组合起来奏出的音乐都比不上兄弟姐妹或父亲母亲亲切的话语那么悦耳。

谈话本身就属于演讲。有许多人在辩论中举足轻重，谈资丰富，在某些时间或地点能呼风唤雨，而一旦身处与自己水平相当的人们中间，他们的说话方式就会变得毫无用武之地。他们就像站在有血有肉的人们面前的机器，没有任何独门的手段去触动人们天性中的东西，这时他们会束手无策、无能为力。一个人在一件乐器面前可以表现得像其主人，而乐器只不过是毫无生命的东西，人拥有灵活的手，他的触动竟然会使无生命的乐器奏出那么精彩、和谐的乐曲！如果一个有生命的人和一件无生命的乐器的力量能震撼观众，那么如果"弦"是鲜活的，人是有活力的，并且他知道怎样用非凡的灵感去触动他们时，观众将会受到多么大的震撼啊！

——比彻

from conversational tones! How seldom does a man dare to acquit himself with pathos and fervor! And the men are themselves mechanical and methodical in the bad way, who are most afraid of the artificial training that is given in the schools, and who so often show by the fruit of their labor that the want of oratory is the want of education.

How remarkable is sweetness of voice in the mother, in the father, in the household! The music of no chorded instruments brought together is, for sweetness, like the music of familiar affection when spoken by brother and sister, or by father and mother.

Conversation itself belongs to oratory. How many men there are who are weighty in argument, who have abundant resources, and who are almost boundless in their power at other times and in other places, but who, when in company among their kind, are exceedingly unapt in their methods. Having none of the secret instruments by which the elements of nature may be touched, having no skill and no power in this direction, they stand as machines before living, sensitive men. A man may be as a master before an instrument; only the instrument is dead; and he has the living hand; and out of that dead instrument what wondrous harmony springs forth at his touch! And if you can electrify an audience by the power of a living man on dead things, how much more should that audience be electrified when the chords are living and the man is alive, and he knows how to touch them with divine inspiration!

—Beecher

每个人都尽最大的努力使自己在社交中讨人喜欢，但通常的情况却是那些一心想在谈话中光芒四射的人往往过甚其词。即使某个人的发言很成功,他也不应该独揽整个谈话（但是通常情况却的确如此）;因为那会破坏谈话的真正实质——谈话嘛就应该几个人一起谈。我们应该努力让谈话像传球那样彼此传来传去，而不是像踢足球带球跑时那样把球控制在自己脚下往前冲。同样,我们要注意使自己的谈话与同伴相适应，不在女士们面前谈论她们不懂的问题，不在乡村法官会议上谈论最新流行的服饰。

然而，给整个谈话笼罩上荒唐气氛的莫过于某些坏习惯,它们极易养成,却难以克服或戒除。为了更真切地展示这些荒诞的习惯，我想列出一些最常见的例子:首先请注意社交中的那些丑角,也就是那些喜欢装模作样和做鬼脸者。他们说每句话都附带着奇怪的鬼脸或姿势；他们赞成必耸肩,反对必甩头;生气必撇嘴,开心必雀跃。他们可以被看作喜剧中既有动作又有台词的滑稽角色；他们以为想让话语有说服力必须加上柔体杂技演员般的动作。这些人应该被惩罚与镜子里的自己

Every one endeavors to make himself as agreeable to society as he can; but it often happens that those who most aim at shining in conversation, overshoot their mark. Tho a man succeeds, he should not (as is frequently the case) engross the whole talk to himself; for that destroys the very essence of conversation, which is talking together. We should try to keep up conversation like a ball bandied to and fro from one to the other, rather than seize it all to ourselves, and drive it before us like a football. We should likewise be cautious to adapt the matter of our discourse to our company, and not talk Greek before ladies, or of the last new furbelow to a meeting of country justices.

But nothing throws a more ridiculous air over our whole conversation than certain peculiarities easily acquired, but very difficultly conquered and discarded. In order to display these absurdities in a truer light, it is my present purpose to enumerate such of them as are most commonly to be met with; and first to take notice of those buffons in society, the Attitudinarians and Face–makers. These accompany every word with a peculiar grimace or gesture; they assent with a shrug, and contradict with a twisting of the neck; are angry by a wry mouth, and pleased in a caper or minuet step. They may be considered as speaking harlequins; and their rules of eloquence are taken from the posture–master. These should be condemned to converse only in dumb show with their own

演哑剧。还有那些一个劲儿傻笑或假笑的人，说话时脸上的表情很生动，那样子还很难描述——咧着嘴，露出酒窝，似笑非笑。除此之外，还有那些做作的模仿者。他们总是模仿熟人独特的腔调或姿势，但他们却是拙劣的模仿者，就像蹩脚的画家一样，只有把被模仿者的名字写出来，别人才能发现其中的相似之处。

说完那些演说注重动作、主要借用四肢交谈的人，我们要说说那些“自封的专业演说家们”。首先，是那些过分用力地挤压、着重每一个音节的“强调者”。这些演讲者最突出的特点就是清楚的吐字和有力的表达；他们拖长重要之处的“of”和“the”，以及他们认为值得注意的连词“and”。他们看起来十分费力地从喉咙里挤出这些词，并且竭力将他们塞进听众的耳朵里。这就好像用喇叭状的助听器把话灌进聋子的耳朵里；但是我必须承认我也同样厌恶“耳语者”或“低声说话者”。他们似乎以为所有的熟人都是聋子，说话时总是凑到你跟前，就好像要跟你比一比鼻子的大小，还

persons in the looking-glass, as well as the Smirkers and Smilers, who so prettily set off their faces, together with their words, by a *je-ne-sais-quoi* between a grin and a dimple. With these we may likewise rank the affected tribe of mimics, who are constantly taking off the peculiar tone of voice or gesture of their acquaintance, tho they are such wretched imitators, that (like bad painters) they are frequently forced to write the name under the picture before we can discover any likeness.

Next to these whose elocution is absorbed in action, and who converse chiefly with their arms and legs, we may consider the Profest Speakers. And first, the Emphatical, who squeeze, and press, and ram down every syllable with excessive vehemence and energy. These orators are remarkable for their distinct elocution and force of expression; they dwell on the important particulars "of " and "the", and the significant conjunction "and", which they seem to hawk up, with much difficulty, out of their own throats, and to cram them, with no less pain, into the ears of their auditors. These should be suffered only to syringe (as it were) the ears of a deaf man, through a hearing-trumpet; tho I must confess that I am equally offended with the Whisperers or Low-speakers, who seem to fancy all their acquaintance deaf, and come up so close to you that they may be said to measure noses with you, and frequently

总是呼出满嘴臭气，让你难以忍受。我希望让这些不可思议的绅士们离人远一点儿用喇叭筒讲话或者去对着回音廊的墙壁讲话。那些端着尊贵的架子，出口必是名言的“智者”和那些“说话如吹口哨者”或发音永远不清晰的“咕哝者”，倒是可以组合起来开音乐会，那一定很有意思；除了以上这几样“乐器”之外，我还想增添声音洪亮的铜管乐器——“大喊大叫者”，他们问候你健康时的声音不亚于公告传报员的咆哮。

还有“爱闲聊者”，他们婉转的喉咙十分适合在谈话中“说些无关紧要的事”。漂亮女子甜美的嗓音“闲谈时尚”，犹如美妙的音乐。但是如果闲话出自其貌不扬、嗓音粗哑的男人之口，那纯粹是无聊，就像用手摇风琴弹奏快步舞曲既刺耳又不和调。我在以前的一篇文章中说到过“诅咒者”，这里我们说说“半吞半吐的诅咒者”，他们常常一句话分成两句说、总是拐弯抹角，口头的诅咒藏头露尾、吐字含混：“天哪，不过”　“蠢货”、“该死”。还有“粗话大王”以及那些喜欢给人起绰号的人，他们叫人“白菜”、“螃蟹”、“怪小子”、“怪人”或者“臭皮囊”。如果没有翻译，别人很难明白他们在说什么。为了不使读者们厌烦，我不打算一一指出那些说话令人讨厌的人了，也不想特别详述“什么都明白的人”——他们即使是最琐碎的事也说得头头是道，并且出口成章；“什么都要问的人”——他们总是好奇地问现在几点了，天

overcome you with the full exhalations of a foul breath. I would have these oracular gentry obliged to speak at a distance through a speaking–trumpet, or apply their lips to the walls of a whispering–gallery. The Wits who will not condescend to utter anything but a *bon –mot,* and the Whistlers or Tune–hummers, who never articulate at all, may be joined very agreeably together in concert; and to these tinkling cymbals I would also add the sounding brass, the Bawler, who inquires after your health with the bellowing of a town–crier.

The Tattlers, whose pliable pipes are admirably adapted to the "soft parts of conversation", and sweetly "prattling out of fashion", make very pretty music from a beautiful face and a female tongue; but from a rough manly voice and coarse features mere nonsense is as harsh and dissonant as a jig from a hurdy–gurdy. The Swearers I have spoken of in a former paper; but the Half–Swearers, who split and mince, and fritter their oaths into "gad's but", "ad's fish", and "demme", the Gothic Humbuggers, and those who nickname God's creatures, and call a man a cabbage, a crab, a queer cub, an odd fish, and an unaccountable skin, should never come into company without an interpreter. But I will not tire my reader's patience by pointing out all the pests of conversation, nor dwell particularly on the Sensibles, who pronounce dogmatically on the most trivial points, and speak in sentences; the Wonderers, who are always wondering what o'clock it is, or wondering

会不会下雨，月亮什么时候圆；“玩弄语法修辞的人”——他们用各种各样的方式或说法不厌其烦地解释一件事；最后还有“什么也不敢说的人”——他们似乎担心一旦开口说话就会着凉感冒，并且逐字研究教义中的箴言以防出错，因此谈话中只说“是”或“不是”。

通过谈话保持理性交流是我们区别于野兽的重要标志，因此，我们必须努力使这一特有的天赋转变成自己的优势。应该将说话的器官看作互相理解的工具，切忌把它们当成作恶的武器或者愚弄他人的工具。此外，应当竭力戒除细微、可笑的坏习惯，因为它们常有损我们这种宝贵天赋的价值。有的哲学家认为即使是鸟儿和野兽也能通过嘴中发出的声音丝毫不差地互相理解（虽然它们不能说话），而狗哇、猫哇什么的就像不同民族一样都有自己独特的语言。因此，我们可以假定，就像意大利的男男女女能很好地欣赏本国的歌曲那样，意大利的夜莺也能完全理解自己那片树林中的各种鸟叫声；威斯特伐利亚的公猪鼻孔发出的咕哝声和高地德语区的居民说的话一样有其意义；荷兰堤坝上青蛙的叫声就像低地荷兰人喋喋不休的话一样可以理解。即便如此，我们仍然可以

whether it will rain or no, or wondering when the moon changes; the Phraseologists, who explain a thing by all that, or enter into particulars, with this and that and t′other; and lastly, the Silent Men, who seem afraid of opening their mouths lest they should catch cold, and literally observe the precept of the Gospel, by letting their conversation be only yea and nay.

The rational intercourse kept up by conversation is one of our principal distinctions from brutes. We should, therefore, endeavor to turn this peculiar talent to our advantage, and consider the organs of speech as the instruments of understanding; we should be very careful not to use them as the weapons of vice, or tools of folly, and do our utmost to unlearn any trivial or ridiculous habits, which tend to lessen the value of such an inestimable prerogative. It is, indeed, imagined by some philosophers, that even birds and beasts (tho without the power of articulation) perfectly understand one another by the sounds they utter; and that dogs, cats, etc., have each a particular language to themselves, like different nations. Thus it may be supposed that the nightingales of Italy have as fine an ear for their own native woodnotes as any signor or signora for an Italian air; that the boars of Westphalia gruntle as expressively through the nose as the inhabitants in High German; and that the frogs in the dykes of Holland croak as intelligibly as the natives jabber their Low Dutch. However this may be, we may consider those whose tongues hardly seem to be

把那些语无伦次，不能使人们的交谈正常进行的人看作是在模仿不同动物的语言。这样一来，就像“喋喋不休者”与猴子之间，“瞎扯者”与鹦鹉之间有相似之处就绝不是偶然的了。“咕哝者”和“咆哮者”就好比爱嗷嗷叫的猪；“怒吼者”就像总是龇牙咧嘴却从不咬人的狗；“性情暴烈者”就像一种野猫，不愿意被人抚摸，但高兴时又会发出愉快的呜呜声；“抱怨者” 好比尖叫的猫头鹰；总是重复同样无聊故事的“讲故事者”就好比布谷鸟。只管竖起耳朵陶醉地听自己难听的叫声的诗人比傻驴好不到哪儿去。批评家们大多是喜欢吐信子的毒蛇，其中一些死背了一点儿专业术语却又一知半解的人就无异于喳喳叫的喜鹊了。而我自己，朝着全城的人喔喔地叫了三年，可能会被读者认为是只谷仓场院里的公鸡；但是现在我要告诉他们两个星期后的今天他们所听到的将是我最后要说的话，因此我希望他们将我看作是一只在辞世之际放声高歌的天鹅。

——珂珀

不给人予痛苦几乎成了对绅士的定义。目前看来，这一描述是准确而精练的。绅士的主要时间

under the influence of reason, and do not keep up the proper conversation of human creatures, as imitating the language of different animals. Thus, for instance, the affinity between Chatterers and Monkeys, and Praters and Parrots, is too obvious not to occur at once; Grunters and Growlers may be justly compared to Hogs; Snarlers are Curs that continually show their teeth, but never bite; and the Spitfire passionate are a sort of wild cats that will not bear stroking, but will purr when they are pleased. Complainers are Screech–Owls; and Story–Tellers, always repeating the same dull note, are Cuckoos. Poets that prick up their ears at their own hideous braying are no better than Asses. Critics in general are venomous Serpents that delight in hissing, and some of them who have got by heart a few technical terms without knowing their meaning are no other than Magpies. I, myself, who have crowed to the whole town for near three years past may perhaps put my readers in mind of a Barnyard Cock; but as I must acquaint them that they will hear the last of me on this day fortnight, I hope that they will then consider me as a Swan, who is supposed to sing sweetly at his dying moments.

—Cowper

It is almost a definition of a gentleman to say that he is one who never inflicts pain. This description is both refined, and, so far as it goes, accurate. He is mainly occupied in merely

就是用来帮周围的人清除妨碍自由自在行事的障碍。他跟他们一起行动，而不是自己首先采取行动。可以认为绅士的作用给人的个性发挥提供了舒适与方便的环境——那就好像提供了一把舒服的椅子或一炉温暖的炉火，可以驱散寒冷和疲劳，虽然即使没有它们大自然也提供了休息和保持体温的方法。真正的绅士同样应小心地避免自己的言行给同伴带来刺激或失望——避免任何观点冲突或感情抵触，避免让他们产生压抑、怀疑、郁闷或怨恨。他最关心的应该是使每一个人都感到无拘无束。他关注身边的每一位同伴，温和地对待害羞的人，文雅地对待冷漠的人，宽容地对待可笑的人。他清楚自己是在和谁说话；竭力防止可能惹恼人的不合时宜的影射和话题；在谈话中他很少引人注目，也绝不会使人感到疲倦。他援手助人却并不把这种恩惠放在心上，明明是在帮别人却好像是别人在帮自己。除非万不得已，他从不谈论自己，也不会反驳别人来为自己辩护；对于流言蜚语，他充耳不闻；对于妨碍自己的人也不轻易追究，总是一切朝好的方面看。在争论中，他从不斤

removing the obstacles which hinder the free and unembarrassed action of those about him, and he concurs with their movements rather than takes the initiative himself. His benefits may be considered as parallel to what are called the comforts or conveniences in arrangements of a personal nature—like an easy chair or a good fire, which do their best in dispelling cold and fatigue, tho nature provides both means of rest and animal heat without them. The true gentleman in like manner carefully avoids whatever may cause a jar or a jolt in the mind of those with whom he is cast—all clashing of opinion or collision of feeling, all restraint or suspicion or gloom or resentment, his great concern being to make every one at ease and at home. He has his eyes on all his company, he is tender toward the bashful, gentle toward the distant, and merciful toward the absurd. He can recollect to whom he is speaking; he guards against unseasonable allusions or topics which may irritate; he is seldom prominent in conversation, and never wearisome. He makes light of favors when he does them, and seems to be receiving when he is conferring. He never speaks of himself except when compelled, never defends himself by a mere retort; he has no ears for slander or gossip, is scrupulous in imputing motive to those who interfere with him, and interprets everything for the best. He is never mean or little in his disputes,

斤计较，或得理不让人，或进行人身攻击、冷嘲热讽，也不含沙射影。他深谋远虑，遵循古代圣人的箴言，即对待敌人要怀着“也许有一天他将成为朋友”的心态。他非常理智，能做到宠辱不惊。他经常忙不及履，无暇把受到的伤害记在心中，同时也懒得因怨恨而耿耿于怀；他有耐心、宽容、凡是顺其自然；他能忍受痛苦，因为痛苦总是不可避免；他泰然接受亲人的逝去，因为那无法挽回；他坦然面对死亡，因为那是命中注定。即使卷入某种争论，其出色的才智也足以使他避免粗率无礼。而那些脑子虽好却缺少教养的人才会粗率无礼，那样的人像钝的兵器那样撕扯削砍、磨磨唧唧，而不能干脆利落地解决争论。那些人常抓不住争辩的要点，为琐碎问题浪费精力，对对手抱有成见，使问题变得比原来更复杂。绅士的观点有可能对也有可能错，但绝对通情达理、公正诚实；他的话朴实且有说服力，简洁且果断。我们再也找不到比他更坦率、更周到、更宽容的人了。他能为对手着想，为他们的错误辩解。他清楚人类理智的力量、职责和极限，同样也清楚它的弱点。即便他是无信仰者，也不会嘲笑或反对宗教，这是因为他思想深邃，心胸开阔；他大智若愚，不会固执己见或不忠不义。他

never takes unfair advantage, never mistakes personalities or sharp sayings for arguments, or insinuates evil which he dare not say out. From a long-sighted prudence, he observes the maxim of the ancient sage, that we should ever conduct ourselves toward our enemy as if he were one day to be our friend. He has too much good sense to be affronted at insults. He is too well employed to remember injuries and too indolent to bear malice. He is patient, forbearing, and resigned on philosophical principle; he submits to pain because it is inevitable, to bereavement, because it is irreparable, and to death because it is his destiny. If he engages in controversy of any kind, his disciplined intellect preserves him from the blundering discourtesy of better, perhaps, but less educated minds, who, like blunt weapons, tear and hack instead of cutting clean, who mistake the point in argument, waste their strength on trifles, misconceive their adversary, and leave the question more involved than they find it. He may be right or wrong in his opinion, but he is too clear-headed to be unjust; he is as simple as he is forcible, and as brief as he is decisive. Nowhere shall we find greater candor, consideration, indulgence; he throws himself into the minds of his opponents, he accounts for their mistakes. He knows the weakness of human reason as well as its strength, its province, and its limits. If he can be an unbeliever, he will be too profound and large-minded to ridicule religion or to act against it; he is too wise to be a dogmatist or fanatic in his

敬重虔诚与奉献。即使自己不赞成，也会因为其历史悠久、风景秀丽或于他人有用而支持一些教会机构；他尊敬牧师，虽然他认为减少宗教的神秘性是好的，但他绝不会抨击或谴责这种神秘性。他认同宗教的宽恕精神，这不仅是因为他的人生观告诉他要公正地看待所有信仰，也是源于良好教养带来的那种高尚而温和的情感。

——纽曼

infidelity. He respects piety and devotion; he even supports institutions as venerable, beautiful or useful, to which he does not assent; he honors the ministers of religion, and it contents him to decline its mysteries without assailing or denouncing them. He is a friend of religious toleration, and that not only because his philosophy has taught him to look on all forms of faith with an impartial eye, but also from the gentleness and effeminacy of feeling which is attendant on civilization.

—Newman